I0202693

Scanning the Arena

VIEWING THE CONTEST
FROM A BOX SEAT

ROBERT V. WILLS

LEMON LANE PRESS • SANTA ANA, CALIFORNIA

Copyright 2018 © Robert V. Wills

ISBN 978-0-9961675-9-8 (print)

Also available in e-book

All rights reserved. No part of this book may be reproduced or transmitted in any form or by any means, electronic or mechanical, including photocopying, recording by an information recording and retrieval system, without express written permission from the publisher.

Lemon Lane Press
1811 Beverly Glen Drive
Santa Ana, CA 92705
(714) 544-0344

www.maralys.com

Cover & book design: Sue Campbell Book Design
Cover image: Ninetails, depositphotos.com

Praise for *Scanning the Arena*

Bob Wills' series of essays in *Scanning the Arena* make fascinating reading. His insightful and timely essays cover a spectrum of topics from the political and economic state of the planet to the social and ethical systems of the day. Thought-provoking … they're worth your time.

> William Kropp, Ph.D.,
> Research physicist

Prepare to have your lapels grabbed by this pithy volume! You'll find opinionated, witty, thought-provoking perspectives generated by a razor-sharp intellect focused on politics, the human condition, and the future of our country and our world.

> Jevelyn Yonchar, M.D.

After years of hearing this brilliant lawyer's wisdom and insights, I'm happy to see it down on paper for all of us to share. A treat to read an original viewpoint.

> Elaine Weinberg, J.D.

Robert Wills' essays are consistently thought-provoking, covering a wide and varied range of subjects. His writing style is succinct and compelling. Based on the author's life experiences, and coupled with his wide range of knowledge and quick recall of facts, the essays always ring true. I eagerly await each new one!

> Linda R. Mayeda, M.A., Stanford University

Scanning the Arena gives the reader a look into the mind of a great thinker. Bob's thoughts on young and old, red and blue, small pleasures and great calamities, are a gift to behold. With his mixture of sharp prose and just plain common sense, you will find yourself savoring these essays, and thinking of them long after you've finished this book.

Beth Strayer Handweiler, C.S.R.

It is always a treat to receive Bob Wills' writings. Bob peels back the layers of some of our most pressing topics and offers unique and insightful perspectives. His observations are intellectually stimulating, viewpoint enhancing and entertaining. We never miss the opportunity to read each one!

Tom and Tammy Hunt

When we open the mailbox to discover an envelope from Bob Wills, we know it's going to be a great day with an amazing read! His 'Reflection and Retrospection' Series contains keen and sometimes scary observations and insights about world events, politics, and human behavior. Please keep them coming!!!

Kathy and Carl Greenwood

Well-written and researched, sometimes reflective and melancholic, often direct and audacious, always intelligent and thought-provoking, his essays, for a moment, stop me in my tracks. Make me think. Make me wonder. Make me say out loud: Amen!

Bernardine Wilcox, M.P.T.

CONTENTS

Acknowledgements

Show me a wordsmith and I'll show you someone who doesn't suffer editing lightly. The fact that I allowed Maralys to tinker a bit with some of my sentences in these pieces is no testimony to my good nature. Rather, it's a tribute to her evolved skill as an editor and manuscript polisher. And a payback for some of the nuggets I've planted in her nineteen books.

Maralys also runs the computer in this house and got my prose to the printer in apple pie order. So she gets double points for editing and production.

Brad Hagen gets one Brownie point for buying an Alpha Smart keyboard for Maralys, only because I commandeered it and do all my writing on it.

Sue Campbell provided invaluable design and production for this third little volume of essays. She knows more about book design and production than we will ever know and we are grateful for her help.

A Plunder So Slick That Few Notice

THE AVERAGE PERSON PROBABLY realizes that a lot of American CEO's make seven figures per year, not including stock options, but even sophisticated investors have no idea of the extent of the corporate plunder. They don't know that the CEO's of large corporations all make an EIGHT figure salary, and the Microsoft CEO, not a familiar name, made $84,309,000 last year. That's $39,919 per hour for a 40 hour week.

I'm looking at a list of 50 CEO's of American companies, and the average 2014 compensation seems to be somewhere in the $19,000,000 range. That's about $1,600,000 per month, and $9,000 per hour for a 40 hour week. Compare that to the hourly wage of a middle management guy who is working as hard or harder than his CEO—$100,000 per year and $47 per hour. Or a production line worker, at $40,000 per year and $19 per hour.

There's only one possible reason for American CEO's getting these obscene amounts from corporate treasuries, and that reason is because they CAN. The only union in this country that isn't under active political attack is the unseen, stealth CEO's union, which has succeeded in leap-frogging CEO salaries by claiming that CEO's are expected to be miracle workers and the whole future of the company rests on their shoulders. Therefore each corporation feels it has to outbid the others for a charismatic, track-proven CEO, and they have to meet his ever-higher salary and stock option demands or lose him.

Thus the compensation of the Microsoft CEO went to $84,309,000 and the compensation of the Oracle CEO (and Founder) went to $67,261,000 and the salary of the Qualcomm CEO went to $60,740,000. Even genial Bob Iger drew $43,702,000 at Disney last year.

Strangely, only the CEO of an American corporation is considered to be the be-all, end-all employee. The salaries of other executives have risen, often to 7 figures, and middle managers to 6 figures. But drop down to the assembly line and service personnel and you see no such trend. In fact, the economists tell us that the average American worker has been losing ground until recently because of unemployment

And anti-union pressure. Even the pensions of lower echelon employees are coming under attack—because of irresponsible past optimism and underfunding.

I don't see any forces on the horizon that would halt the obscene CEO domino effect. No Federal or State laws are violated by outlandish executive salaries. Individual shareholders like me simply scan the annual reports and send in signed proxies. The large shareholders, like funds, don't rock the boat if the company is on track, or suggest bidding for a new (and more expensive) CEO if it isn't.

There are no protesters or "occupiers" to target CEO salaries. The protesters don't even know how outrageous the scenario is. They target the gross disparity of American income in general—but don't know what to do about it.

What's your solution to the CEO compensation fiasco? If you don't have one, maybe the sky's the limit.

4/30/15

An American Racket that's Both Legal and Profitable

Few U.S. citizens other than corporate lawyers and corporate executives are aware of a legal scheme that very quietly costs American consumers hundreds of millions of dollars a year and is not only legal but administered by Federal Courts themselves.

It's called class action litigation and its practitioners hold themselves out as legal watchdogs over corporate "governance" by bringing lawsuits in Federal Court against corporations and corporate executives who allegedly violated laws and regulations governing corporate transactions. The lawsuits are filed by law firms that specialize in corporate law and look over the shoulders of corporate management when publicly traded stocks are involved in a merger or acquisition or financing.

The lawyers and their accountants scrutinize the financial statements and the shareholder communications to see if management played a little fast and loose with shareholders, or executives were "unjustly enriched", or some I's weren't dotted or t's crossed in the SEC requirements for mergers and acquisitions or financial transactions.

The stated goal of the class action suits is to make sure that transactions involving publicly traded stock are "fair, just, and equitable" for the company's shareholders. The actual result of most of these lawsuits is 1) a colossal headache for management involved, 2) major legal and accounting expense for the company to respond to the litigation, 3) 6 or 7 figure attorneys fees for the attacking law firm, as allowed by the Court, 4) 5 figure reimbursement of costs for the attacking law firm, 5) a stipulation revising some of the corporation's shareholder communications, including financial data, and 6) occasionally, but now less frequently, a division among shareholders of a six or seven figure settlement amount to be paid by the company.

I have held publicly traded stocks for over 50 years and have half a file drawer full of class action files where I went to the trouble of filing a claim. It's such an ordeal, gathering and photocopying stock transaction documents from years ago and completing an affidavit, that I'm sure most shareholders learned, as I did over the years, that the payments to the shareholders rarely exceed 3 figures and often amount to 2 figures (under $100), so it's hardly worth the time and trouble to file a claim, even though my holdings were usually 500 or more shares of stock.

But as the notices of the class action suits come in, I circle two items: the amount of any settlement amount, if any, and the attorneys fees requested by the attacking law firm. I have found a trend in the last several years. The settlements more often than not describe some accounting corrections or explanations and promises of good corporate governance in the future—but no payments to shareholders. Just 6 or 7 figure attorneys fees to the attacking law firm for its high-minded, public-spirited good work.

I now wonder if the Federal Judges reviewing and approving these class action settlements have seen the trend and ever consider the obvious cost to the corporation, and thereby the public that buys its products. Not to mention the shareholders who were supposed to be the beneficiaries of the lawsuits, but who received nothing but assurances and sweet talk while the corporate treasury took a hit.

I suppose that having these legal foxes prowling outside the hen house does keep corporate executives a little more on the straight and narrow than otherwise. I would hate to think that SEC supervision was all the protection shareholders have. Under George W. Bush the SEC was either asleep at the switch or on a leash, and even under Obama they don't scare executives much.

So maybe the Judges feel that someone has to look out for the poor, defenseless shareholders and, since the government doesn't seem to do it, why not let a few big city attorneys get rich by guarding the corporate hen house?

5/7/15

From "Snake Pits" to Skid Row: Charming Ronnie's Legacy

THE REPUBLICAN CONSERVATIVE WING and the Libertarian stalwarts are all anxious to see a smiling Ronald Reagan on American coins and other memorabilia. They still buy the story that he won the Cold War, fought Communism to a standstill on all fronts, and limited the size of the California and Federal governments. Most of it is urban myth, but idolatry dies hard and Reagan fans aren't burdened by any hard economic or political facts.

What Ronnie's rooters have forgotten, or never noticed, is that California passed the largest tax increase in any State's history while he was Governor, and the Federal deficit increased sharply while he was President, both flying smack in the face of his campaign rhetoric promising smaller government with better management.

Reagan started out as Governor with a promise to cut California spending by 10 percent, but had to abandon that goal rapidly once he got educated on the job. His background as a sports announcer and movie actor gave him zero knowledge of government, and because of his basic skepticism about government, he surrounded himself in Sacramento with novices and amateurs, this per one of his chief novices, Lyn Nofziger, his Communications Director.

Reagan soon found that instead of shrinking California government, he needed a huge tax increase and he ended up compromising amicably with a Democratic legislature for 8 years.

But one government program that Reagan had distaste for was a system of mental hospitals housing approximately 22,000 patients when he took office. It had been slimmed down already from 37,500 patients under Governor Edmund Brown, but Reagan, like Nixon, was skeptical about psychiatrists and psychiatric theory. He once portrayed mental patients as mostly alcoholics and ne'er-do-wells, and completed the process of closing down the last of California's mental hospitals, with disastrous long term effects.

Reagan was supported to some extent in that particular government shutdown by a phenomenon occurring in the field of Pharmacology, which, in turn, produced a wave of premature, unjustified optimism in the field of Psychiatry. The supposed panacea was the introduction and promotion of a panoply of new tranquilizer drugs like Valium and Librium, and also some new antipsychotic drugs like Thorazine. The American Psychiatric Association gave Reagan all the help he needed by testifying optimistically in Congressional hearings that the new drugs offered such great promise that the mental hospitals, then often referred to as "snake pits" and "loony bins," might no longer be necessary. There was talk of the states setting up "community clinics" to control mental illness on an outpatient basis with the new drugs.

Ironically, one of Jimmy Carter's last pieces of legislation in 1979 was The Mental Health Systems Act, calling for Federal grants to the states for dealing with mental illness. Ronald Reagan refused those grants before the ink was dry on the federal law and dismantled the remaining California mental hospitals and relied on the medical profession to deal with the problem through community clinics.

Another blow to California hospitalization for mental illness came in 1967 in the form of the Lanterman-Petris-Short Act, which abolished involuntary hospitalization for mental illness except in extreme cases. That is still the law, supported by California's famous "72 hour hold" and "14 day hold" provisions in the Welfare and Institutions Code. These procedures allow medical or police authorities to hospitalize individuals who are manifestly a threat to themselves or the public, but they are rarely used because the requirements are strict and the civil liberties organizations have endowed individuals "held" with numerous rights and protections, including habeas corpus procedures.

The dismantling of California's mental hospitals in the 60's and the call for community clinics to fill the gap created a whole new business, one to which Reagan's friends and campaign supporters flocked. The business was, and is, for-profit board and care facilities financed by insurance and families willing to pay for unloading a disturbed family member. One called Beverly Enterprises, set up by Reagan's pals, ran 38 of them. So the real beneficiaries of the death knell for mental hospitals were the drug industry with its new panoply of drugs, and the for-profit board and care facilities that filled in for the state-run community clinics that never saw the light of day.

It's now all-too-common knowledge that the large numbers of California mentally ill are located in two places, California prisons and California skid rows. The estimates of mentally ill California prisoners start at 30 percent and run upward from there, but there are no means in California prisons for diagnosing (or treating) mental illness, so exact numbers are impossible.

Similar statistics are used for transients, vagrants, and the homeless in general. No one wants them and no one treats them—until they are caught committing a crime. Then they are incarcerated without diagnosis or medication unless they behave so psychotically and menacingly that they are held in a hospital for 72 hours and then released or sent to one of the few facilities for the criminally insane.

There are lots of reasons why California prisons and homeless shelters and skid rows are teeming with society's outcasts . Alcohol and drugs play a huge role and needed no help from a grinning Ronnie Reagan. But a lot of the rejects and castoffs are victims of either genetic or drug-induced or alcohol-induced psychosis. And without state-run hospitals and clinics, they aren't going to get treatment or get better. We can just wait until they die off and hope they stay out of sight. Thanks for your help, Ronnie.

5/18/15

(Ref. *NY Times* 10/30/84 *Salon* 9/29/13, E. Fuller Torrey, Oxford Univ. Press, 2014)

FROM BLUE FLU TO BLUE SNOOZE: Can Vigilantes and Posses be Far Behind?

I'VE TOLD ANYONE WHO would listen how American policemen were going to react to the torrent of hatred, ridicule, and hostility they are receiving from 1) the press, 2) lawyers, 3) politicians, 4) social activists, and 5) so-called "minorities" in the "hood". The simple solution: make fewer and fewer arrests for felonies, because 1) arrests involve the most physical and legal trauma, and 2) no cop gets killed, injured, suspended, or sued for failing to apprehend a criminal, even if he has the opportunity. Fewer arrests mean fewer riots, mob scenes, disciplinary hearings, and lawsuits. How many policemen have been called on the carpet or pilloried in the press for failing to arrest a perpetrator, even if the crime occurred in his presence? Only the victim, not the whole neighborhood, cries foul when the officer fails to pursue or arrest. The press never hears about it.

But it didn't take the press long to start talking

about a reduced arrest rate and an increasing crime rate. The two go hand in hand, especially if the goons and thugs and thieves among us see the trend. And although the criminal element in our society may not be the intellectual cream of the population—except for white collar/financial con artists—they are smart enough to sniff a reduced surveillance and a reduced inclination to apprehend.

So you can safely predict an increase in property crimes, including burglary, and domestic violence and personal assault and battery, all crimes that occur outside police presence and tend to get into he-said she-said controversies.

Police everywhere feel that they are on trial and going to be second-guessed on everything they do, by the press, by defense lawyers, by the "minority" majorities in the ghettos and the projects, and even by their superiors. They might get a commendation for pulling someone out of a burning car or apartment, but they won't get any kudos for an arrest of a felon or the slaying or wounding of a homicidal maniac.

So why risk life, limb, or salary in apprehending a cop-hating psychopath? It might be your job to do it, but it may not be your best move if you care about the future.

One American trend is a move in the direction of the old American West. Americans are buying guns in record numbers, both because of fear of killers or terrorists in our midst and because of fear of increased gun control laws. I wonder if the trend to what I would call Blue Snooze will bring back the age of vigilantes and posses if a crime wave gets rampant and some gun freaks call for "citizen" action. Remember, the often-misquoted Second Amendment does refer to "A well-regulated Militia being necessary to the security of a free state ...."

So keep your boots and spurs ready for the call. And remember where you heard it first.

6/7/15

What Happens If A 'Supreme' Slips Into Dementia?

O F THE TEN MOST powerful individuals in U.S. government nine sit on the U.S. Supreme Court. The tenth, the U.S. President, can be removed after 4 years if the citizenry is dissatisfied, and can be almost stymied by Congress in the meanwhile. Or he can be impeached by Congress if convicted by the Senate "for treason, bribery, or other high Crimes and Misdemeanors".

Three Presidents have faced articles of impeachment by the House of Representatives, but none have been convicted by the Senate and removed from office in 225 years (two, Nixon and Clinton, were in our lifetime).

The decisions of the Supreme Court actually impact our lives as much as anything Congress or the President may ordain—witness 2 decisions just this week—so let's take a look at how we could get rid of a Justice who, serving for life, becomes demonstrably demented, obfuscated, or incapacitated.

First of all, where does it say that a Supreme Court Justice sits for life? The answer lies presumably in Article III, Section 1 of the Constitution, which states "The Judges...shall hold their Offices during good behaviour." There is no definition of "good behaviour" anywhere in the document, and that term might have a much broader scope in 2015 than it did in 1787. But, in any case, the term as been taken to mean for life to this point, so we move on to the more complex question; how do we remove a Justice who has clearly "lost it" mentally or cannot function physically?

The Constitution does not address the question directly, but, in 1805, when Congress got very angry with Justice Samuel Chase, someone decided that Article II, Section 4 provided an answer. It states that "The President, Vice President, and all civil Officers of the United States shall be removed from Office on Impeachment for, and Conviction of, Treason, Bribery, or other high Crimes and Misdemeanors." Justice Chase was impeached by the house, but acquitted by the Senate, so no Justice has ever been removed from the Court.

But note that the impeachment grounds in Article II say absolutely nothing about disability, mental or physical, or even misconduct not falling in the category of "high Crimes or Misdemeanors." There is still great debate over whether any misconduct or malpractice not falling within the definition of a crime is proper ground for impeachment. The fact that "misdemeanor" had no specific meaning in 1787 only adds to the confusion. Bill Clinton's only "crime" in the bill of impeachment brought by his Republican enemies in the House 16 years ago was alleged lying to Congress in a semantic debate over the word "sex." The impeachment obviously failed.

But I find no authority or discussion about any method of removal of a Justice because of physical or mental incapacity. If Article II, Section 4 is the only basis for removal, and if Justices are going to live for 40 or more years after appointment, well into senility and incapacity, I think we have a fascinating problem coming up down the road.

Maybe someone will argue, heroically if not successfully, that "good behaviour" implies mens sana in corpore sana as a condition to a Justice's term. If Antonin Scalia gets any more outraged or rabid, or Clarence Thomas gets any more inarticulate and deferential, then someone should give it a try, or ask Congress to legislate a 2015 definition of "good behaviour."

6/26/15

LIKE A SWISS WATCH

IT'S FASCINATING TO WATCH a group of individuals so thoroughly organized and disciplined that they operate like a well-oiled machine. Traditional examples are military drill teams, college marching bands, and chorus lines. A top flight football team often demonstrates crisp timing and flow, too.

Any major symphony orchestra exhibits the ultimate timing and coordination once the conductor starts the flow with his baton. I'm always impressed in Segerstrom or Meng Hall to see so many talented and intelligent humans exercising 100 percent discipline and control for up to 40 minutes at a time, with only a rare blue note or cadence miss. To me that demonstration of precision and focus represents an ultimate in human refinement and maturity.

There are few other events in our boisterous, restless democracy where coordination, focus, and discipline produce anything like a symphony or a concerto.

So imagine my amazement at discovering another outstanding example of human coordination and discipline in a popular fast food restaurant at rush hour. It happened quite accidentally and only because I got us a booth that had a clear view of what turned out to be a human beehive. The kitchen at In 'N Out in Tustin Market Place is very much like a beehive—crowded, full of bodies, and seemingly chaotic.

It turned out that there were 18 employees operating at breakneck speed in an L-shaped area no bigger than a Lemon Heights kitchen. All but a row of six griddle cooks were performing two or more functions, at the order counter, at the window, at French fry and other machines, at the delivery counter, in and out of the supply room in the back and customer eating areas outside the kitchen.

Even though the menu is wisely and historically simple, there were literally dozens of functions being performed, with 12 of the 18 multiracial, energetic crew shifting rapidly from task to task in a non-collision ebb and flow.

When a middle-aged worker named Jeff (name tag) attended to some supplies near us, I asked him how they manage to avoid collisions in such close quarters. He smiled and indicated they do have a few.

It took only a few more minutes of observation to determine that Jeff was not only the oldest employee— he was the manager of all 18. He moved swiftly from work station to work station, talked quickly with workers on the fly, got supplies, and did every function except grilling himself.

In one area no bigger than 20 square feet, orders were gathered, segregated between counter and drive up window, bagged or trayed, then moved one way or the other. There were even rapid shifts from food service to the four ordering registers, depending on the size of the ordering line. Such a shift moved Maralys forward ten feet in a hurry.

As we left I told Jeff that we thought his human machine was amazing to watch. What I didn't have time to tell him was how we wish the State and Federal government and most other large institutions could emulate the focus and efficiency we witnessed in his beehive.

7/12/15

"Life Is Short": Forget the Seventh Commandment

You may or may not know about a couple of websites that are aimed at people who are married but interested in an adulterous affair. One of them, Ashley Madison, was in the news this week because its data bank got hacked and millions of subscribers are sweating bullets as a result of a threat by the hackers (The Impact Team) to reveal names, message texts, and credit card data.

There are several amazing aspects of this story and they say a lot about American culture. In the first place, Ashley Madison is such a successful company that I first read about it in either Fortune or Forbes magazine as a booming enterprise that is making truckloads of money. Both Ashley Madison and its sister site, Established Men, are owned by a middle-aged mogul and based in Toronto. The motto of Ashley, promoted online, is " Life is short. Have an affair," so there is nothing ambiguous about the business model.

And apparently the venture has tapped a mother lode in America's duplicitous society, because the hackers are threatening to reveal the names and expressed fantasies of "more than thirty million users of AshleyMadison.com," meaning about 9 percent of the current U.S. population.

Two thoughts come to mind if those numbers are accurate. First, is monogamy in big trouble in a supposedly Judeo-Christian society? Adultery is celebrated in novels and the media as an edgy exception, but here is a corporate pimp making a fortune by promoting it as a commercial diversion, in essence, a marital vacation. And here are millions of Internet denizens expressing their yens and fantasies in emails that were sworn to be securely private, and paying extra to have their transactions deleted. So regardless of how many customers hooked up extra-maritally, we know that millions of married Americans are interested in setting monogamy aside, at least for a trial.

The other thought is that Ashley Madison is a money tree thanks to millions of spouses interested in a lark, but not in abandoning home and hearth—either because of general satisfaction at home or because a divorce would be too painful, too career-damaging, or too expensive. There are lots of reasons not to divorce, but apparently not enough to observe the wedding vows forever.

The next question will be what the deceived spouses will do, once The Impact Team reveals the names and credit card expenses of the "cheating" spouses. There will be some divorce filings, some reconciliations, and a lot of pleas for counseling or arbitration. There may even be some retaliation adultery.

But in any case, it won't be pretty. A lot of aggrieved spouses will be pained, a lot of children hurt, and a lot of attorneys engaged. But the Toronto adultery pimp will be very rich. And may move on to a novel form of pornography.

7/22/15

Trophy Hunters and Other Ego-Deficient Vandals

THE PUBLIC UPROAR OVER the craven slaughter of
Cecil, the Zimbabwan protected lion, is both sur-
prising and encouraging. First, that so many thousand
people in the U.S. and elsewhere care enough about
one prized lion to rally, demonstrate, and demonize
the rich "big white hunter" from Minnesota. His plush
dental practice is now closed for the time being and the
world now knows that other effete Americans seeking
adventure spend lots of money to kill 600 African lions
annually, further reducing the declining population.

What the public doesn't yet know is that hundreds
of lions and tigers are shot on U.S. ranches each year
and, like Cecil, most of them are former roadside zoo
or semi-domesticated big cats that were once smaller,
cuter, and easier to maintain, for photographs or displays. They are accustomed to humans but become too
large and rough for handling—and too expensive to

feed. So they are either sold to "safari" ranchers in the south and west or unloaded on one of the six or seven big cat refuges that endlessly ply me and other "cat" people for contributions.

The reason I hear about all the off-loaded big cats is because I got on the supporter list by making initial contributions to Tiger Creek, Tiger Haven, Wildcat Haven, Noah's Lost Animal Ark, Tiger Preservation Center, Marcan Tiger Preserve, and Keepers of The Wild. They want me not only to keep contributing as they go from crisis to crisis (neighbors, government, cold, heat), but also to sign petitions to Federal authorities aimed at prohibiting the profitable and thriving private hunt business in the U.S. These organizations also lobby, justifiably, to force many states to prohibit the purchase and maintenance of big cats and other wild animals for amusement and pets. They're right— private citizens have no business owning tiger or lion cubs because they all grow up and have to be unloaded on the refuge organizations or the private hunt ranches, where they obviously provide pathetic targets for pathetic humans who pretend they are hunters.

Maybe Cecil's disgraceful slaughter will serve a purpose of some sort. Anything that calls attention to the poacher and hunter decimation of elephants and big cats in Africa and Asia is a good thing. But how do you keep millions of Chinese ignoramuses from buying ivory as art or tiger parts as medicine? How do you keep thousands of American morons from shooting former pets and calling it big game hunting?

And how do you get an American Congress dominated by redneck Tea Partiers to do anything about America's highways and bridges, or America's small export companies, much less private purchase and maintenance of wild animals as pets?

I'm not hopeful, but maybe Sub-Saharan Africans will themselves close the gates on American "big white hunters" and Chinese customers for elephant ivory. Unless they do it themselves, I think our great grand-kids—eleven of them—will see lions, tigers, leopards, and elephants only in books and zoos.

7/30/15

A DARK CRYSTAL BALL

I'M STUDYING A UNITED Nations Population Prospects projection of the world population from 2015 to 2100. I'm hoping that it's wrong, and wrong big time. But I doubt it, and I wouldn't recommend a close look by any of my 10 grandkids or 12 great grandkids. The less they can see over the horizon, the happier they, and their parents, will be.

But someone is going to have to study the projection—and even the current world population—and figure out a method of slowing population growth in the so-called "Third World." Because the next four billion humans to be added to today's 7,300,000,000 are scheduled to arrive in the poorest and least civilized areas of the globe, namely, sub-Saharan Africa and southern Asia. India and China, #1 and #2, will still have almost 24 percent of the population, but Nigeria will have passed the U.S. for #3, Congo will be #5, and five of the top 10 populations will be in sub-Saharan

Africa, the least developed and least promising region of the globe. Pakistan (#6) and Indonesia (#7) don't inspire much confidence in a civilized society, either.

Aside from nuclear holocaust, an unattractive but increasingly possible solution (Al Qaeda, ISIS,et al), the only hope I see for a civilized, stable globe in the next 40 or 50 years is an epic breakthrough in birth control and family planning, both a technical and a cultural revolution.

Some sort of revolution is certainly coming—take a look at the North African and Middle Eastern army of refugees invading southern Europe —but the only beneficial revolution will be technical—cheap and easily administered birth control medication—and cultural, a rejection of retrogressive religion and emancipation of the female population in Africa and Asia. I have a lot more confidence in our biotechnical and pharmacological pioneers than in the world's political leaders, who are hamstrung by obsolete religious and social dogma.

Ironically, the same conservative stalwarts who warn us about Armageddon—but who oppose family planning, abortion, and strong government regulation – provide the greatest risk of population Armageddon in this century. That Armageddon will be brought on by starvation, water wars, revolution and/or armed conflict, nuclear or otherwise.

One of these days I would like to hear the conservative Republican or Muslim take on population projections. They probably pooh pooh them, along with climate change data. Is there any solution in the Bible or the Koran? Will God or Allah step in and solve the problem if the population actually reaches 11,200,000,000?

Or should we rely on scientists and political pragmatists who abandon ancient lore and metaphysics? We know the answer. But do they?

8/29/15

But What About All Those Children?

IRECENTLY READ AN article by an Israeli warning Europe that Muslims don't amalgamate into non-Muslim society, and, because of their far-higher birth rate, they have the potential to ultimately change European culture. He pointed to examples of non-amalgamation in France and Sweden.

I'm sure he is right as rain, and his warning comes as hundreds of thousands of Syrian and North African Muslims are literally invading Europe, aiming for the wealthier—and more tolerant—countries of Northern Europe, Germany, Denmark, France, and Sweden. Please note that the Muslim hordes do not head for the Middle Eastern Muslim countries, far closer than Sweden and Germany—but far less tolerant of migrants, refugees, and other potential drains on resources and threats to stability. The migrants know that the Muslim countries are not havens of charity, tolerance, and Christian good-heartedness like the Western European countries are.

That is, good-hearted to a point. I wondered when the two primary targets, Germany and Austria, would wake up to the size of the invasion and their domestic opposition to it, then stem the flood at the borders. The tough administration of Croatia finally voiced the awakening this week: "We have to have hearts, but we must also have brains …".

I have had great misgivings about the mass migration from the outset. Greece, Italy, and Spain already have massive economic problems, without hordes of impecunious migrants. Turkey, being tough and Muslim, has already dodged the bullet. Croatia and Hungary got swamped—being on the path to the promised Teutonic lands—and have spent millions trying to close the door. Italy got hordes from North Africa, but did not have a feasible path to Austria and Germany (picture the Alps). Kindly Jordan, right next door to Syria and Somalia, got overrun by more than a million refugees—who live in miserable refugee camps in the desert—before closing its border.

My wife and all the other tender-hearted American ladies ask, "Then what's the solution? Look at all those children and eager young men." I don't have an answer for them, but I certainly sympathize with the most evolved nations in Europe saying "Enough already. We can't admit endless hordes of Arabs and

North Africans when their Muslim neighbors in the Middle East and Africa turn their oil-rich backs and shut the door."

I know what the long term solution is, and has been for decades. That is obviously universal and thoroughly affordable birth control. But both the male-dominated Muslim societies and the Catholic church are obstacles to any real solution. So prepare for more razor-wire boundaries, military skirmishes, and rioting violence in the short term. It isn't going to be pretty in Germany, Austria, et al—or elsewhere.

9/20/15

MADE-TO-ORDER STATISTICS

SIXTY-SIX YEARS AGO, AS a UCLA graduate student, I wrote an essay called "Party Statistics." The professor liked it enough to read part of it to the class. The theme was that people, including authors of serious prose, toss around statistics as gospel when they may well have plucked them out of thin air. They can't be checked, but who is going to argue with real numbers?

The theme is infinitely more relevant today. We are besieged with numbers by every type of media. Start with the endless political polls, with numbers as flimsy as they are unverifiable. Then the science and health pieces, laced with statistics that are supposed to be ironclad because they are science based. But wait six months and see how they change.

The weather forecasters give us percentages that are as changeable as the weather itself. The health advisors tell us our chances of getting cancer from this food or this activity—but wait a year and see how the numbers change.

Even the most prestigious shows, like *NOVA*, *Nature*, and *Frontline*, toss out statistics that are supposed to amaze us, but are just as unverifiable as they are amazing. Let's see someone prove that a dog's olfactory system is "millions" of times as sensitive as ours, or that our cat has several hundred sets of muscles to move his ears. Or that daily bacon increases the incidence of colon cancer by 20 percent. Or that 23 percent of the world's coral is already dead.

Some figures ARE verifiable to be sure. The Dow Jones average is computable. The reduction in water use by a city or the rise in temperature of the Pacific Ocean in a specific area could be checked. But 90 percent (...!) of the figures thrown at us all day long are absolutely unverifiable and probably false. They may show a trend, if offered serially, but beware of any statistics that are offered as genuine when they're based on a poll, an estimate, or a limited sample.

Each week our favorite news magazine, *THE WEEK*, is loaded with statistics in squibs about how many people go to church, how many black youths are in jail, how many teeth are lost to periodontal disease, how many adults have tattoos, how many people use heroin or marijuana. There is scarcely an article without statistics. The same with *TIME*, the *L.A. Times*, the "*Ragister*" and our various medical school publications. We are swamped with statistics that are intended to give an article gravitas. But I take all such statistics as either estimates or opinions. Because I know they won't be—and usually can't be—checked.

Now for the irony. I not only enjoyed statistics in college, and got an "A" in that subject at UCLA, but before UCLA's Law School opened in 1949 I was headed for a Master's degree in Psychology. Guess what my thesis was going to be, "The statistical correlation between cigarette smoking and lack of breast feeding as a child."

Cigarette smoking was at its peak after WWII and breast feeding had fallen way out of favor. I'm sure I could have shown a positive correlation between the two trends, but the LSAT exam came along and saved me from a brief flurry of sociological fame and a life-time of limited means.

11/9/15

Cashing in on America's Simpletons

Every time I watch an automobile or movie or pharmaceutical ad on TV, I ask myself, "What moron, what juvenile was that thing aimed at?" Nobody I know is that dumb or that childish.

Then I realize that some ad agency or some movie producer spent a lot of money to get that thirty seconds of time on national TV, aimed at millions of viewers, and if they all reacted as I did, a lot of money has been wasted and the ad designer's job is in deep jeopardy.

But then the ads keep coming, month after month, and get goofier or more moronic all the time, so I have to assume that it must be ME that's out of alignment. Maybe the American audience is, in fact, simple minded or juvenile and the ad agencies and movie producers are smarter than I am.

Which they are. They have to be, because they are spending millions of dollars on these inane or violent scenes, over and over, so they must be working. People are buying those cars, those drugs, those Carl's cheese-burgers, and those movie tickets. Because the ads did their work and the agents and producers kept their jobs.

So what the TV ads are telling us is that the average American TV watcher is either a simpleton, a gull, or a juvenile, and I just don't know him or her. Surely everyone I know, everyone in my law school class, my neighborhood, my family, our discussion group, is not a target for TV ads. We are a rogue group, a fringe group, a non-target group. We simply aren't in the mainstream of America.

The advertising moguls and movie producers know America better than I do. And that's scary, because the goofy simplicity and raw violence portrayed in those ads tell me that our precious democracy is in shaky hands.

11/22/15

DECEMBER, 2015

'TIS THE SEASON TO be jolly, Tra La La La La La La La La. However, it's a little hard to be jolly with the world in turmoil, clowns and rednecks running for U.S. President, and very dark clouds just over the horizon. And we're not the jolly type, anyhow. Besides, this isn't a Christmas letter in any sense of the word.

What we are is fortunate and grateful for another bountiful year. Trips to Wyoming, Kauai, the Rhine River countries, and Scotland provided all the excitement we need in our eighties, and blue ribbon medical care solved a couple of medical problems. I'm not used to running around in five countries with a stent in my left ureter, but all's well that ends well.

If you can believe it, Maralys cranked out two books this year, the first a collection of her best tales and the second as a co-writer of a book on breast care and surgery. The co-author is a prominent breast surgeon in Orange County who definitely needed professional writing help, and got it. The book should be out in 2016.

A year after Brad's death Tracy has Video Resources in good health and Dane is rapidly learning to be a video producer himself. Chris joined a large group of Orange County's best orthopedic surgeons for his pre-retirement years. He and Betty Jo spend a lot of time at their much updated ranch between Murietta and Camp Pendleton, an hour and a half from here. And Kenny settled a couple of big malpractice cases that will allow him and Melanie to continue the Good Life.

If you want to keep your Holiday glow, you might want to skip to the last paragraph of this piece because I'm gazing into a murky crystal ball here. Only fellow crystal ball gazers should proceed.

We still see two major threats for our 12 great grandchildren. The first is religious fanaticism, of the type represented by America's Radical Right and Islam's bellicose radicals. We have our brand of evangelical stalwarts and the billion and a half Muslims have theirs, all dedicated to imposing their dogma on atheists, agnostics, moderates, liberals and "infidels".

Thanks to George W. Bush and his two rabid coaches, Chaney and Rumsfeld, the West is now looking at guerrilla warfare for years to come. Hopefully history won't mark our idiotic invasion and destruction of Iraq as the starting point for WWIII. Our best chance of preventing that is obviously Special Forces,

Special Ops, and psychological warfare—not conventional military warfare.

The other threat is obviously the overarching problem of overpopulation. Famine, water depletion, revolution, and mass migrations are just over the horizon. And the most ominous repercussions of the 2015 invasion of Europe by Syrian and North African refugees will be the precedent set by the tolerance of the invasion by the bleeding heart European nations. That will be a precedent they will sorely regret in the future.

If you fast forward five or ten years and study the population trends in both the Muslim world and the tropical latitudes—all with out-of-control birth rates—you may see migrations, actually invasions, of millions from the Torrid Zone (47 degrees around the Equator) to the more prosperous (and industrious) nations in the Temperate Zone. The numbers may make 2015s several hundred thousand refugees look like a trial run, a test case. And the result will be a new kind of war, defending whole regions against hordes of desperate invaders. Not a pretty picture for the evangelical Pro-Lifers to contemplate.

If you share my grim geopolitical outlook, you'll recognize two primary causes of the turmoil and/or wars to come: climate and religious obstruction. It's not a coincidence that the wealthiest nations are all in the Temperate Zones of the globe and the poorest nations are in the Torrid Zone and are either Muslim or

Catholic; for example, Brazil, Indonesia, Southern India, the Central African countries, and Central America. Muslims and Catholics in the Third World have by far the highest birth rates and the least access to family planning. Add food shortages and water depletion to that scenario and guess what's going to follow the 2015 invasion of Europe by a few hundred thousand Muslim refugees.

There is obviously a primary solution—birth control and family planning—and hopefully a few far-sighted philanthropists (like Melinda Gates) will use money and pharmacology to address the problem. But the other solution, if there is one, is where our great grandkids come in. The only response to food and water shortages will have to be technological—vast improvements in agriculture, nutrition, and hydrology. The answers may lie in Silicon Valley, Seattle, or Minneapolis, not Washington, D.C. At MIT, CAL TECH, Stanford, Berkeley, Duke, Princeton, and major universities everywhere. Wherever bright minds deal with the future.

But it will have to be helped along by a few rational politicians who have objectivity and a little foresight. And who aren't overwhelmed by the tycoons and lobbyists who have no interest in, or sense of, the future ("blue sky").

I can only hope that our ten grandkids and twelve great grandkids can help to discredit my forecast. In the meanwhile, the Dow is flirting with 18,000, the NASDAQ is over 5,000, the air is a lot cleaner than it was 50 years ago, and we have no suicide bombers in the U.S. as yet. So we do have quite a few blessings to count as we view the tempest from afar.

How Much Longer Will the So-Called Right of Privacy Be a Sacred Cow?

WHERE IN THE U.S. Constitution does it say that every citizen has a right to privacy? When a few schools are bombed after untraceable phone calls, or when a few more massacres are committed with AR-15's after some encrypted social media, you can expect the security agencies to be asking that very question. And if the tech giants continue to refuse access to private electronic communications that are encrypted and erased, you can expect some Federal pressure, if not court action, to cause national safety to trump an individual's privacy.

As any judge or historian knows, civilization involves an evolving conflict between public welfare and individual rights. The Penal and Civil Codes are full of examples of society's limitation of individual rights. One of my personal themes has always been that personal liberties will always shrink as population density increases and technology advances. People living ever closer together, with increasing methods of creating friction through various devices—mowers, blowers, stereos, alarms—is a formula for more and more laws and regulations.

But now, because of a shrinking global community, both physically and politically, we have a new threat to personal liberties by the name of national security. Our dedicated enemies are now only an Internet click away, a jet flight across some water, and 100 feet away from about 5,000 miles of the U.S. border. We have been attacked at home and face an increasing threat of domestic violence from home-grown enemies numbering in the thousands. The worst is yet to come from domestic killers now in training electronically and anxious to punish a society they despise.

If a primary function of government is to protect its citizens, how can it do so when thousands of its members are the sworn enemy and are able to communicate at will electronically and telephonically, without any government power to monitor them? It can't, but there is going to be a major showdown very soon between civil rights attorneys, civil liberties groups, and Silicon Valley tech giants on one side and government agencies responsible for so-called homeland security on the other.

The only question in my mind is whether the

right of privacy/civil liberties war will start before or after hundreds of domestic ISIS recruits start wholesale suicide bombing in the U.S. In other words, when we are literally at war.

P.S. The ACLU will search in vain for the word "privacy" in the Constitution.

1/5/16

A Troubled Marriage of Convenience

T HE RELATIONSHIP BETWEEN THE U.S. and China is ever more in the spotlight. It's complex, dynamic, schizophrenic, and bipolar. It's economic, it's cultural, and it's political. And it's a critical factor in the future of our children and grandchildren (ultimately eclipsing the role of Russia and/or India).

Our discussion group recently debated whether China's economic power is looming as a threat or hindrance to U.S. economic health. The Shanghai stock market crashes, so the Dow Jones and NASDAQ falter. The Chinese recession softens the global demand for oil, so the U.S. oil market sinks.

The Chinese bought GE's home appliance business, a Hollywood movie studio, a huge Swiss chemical company ($43 billion), and large chunks of the Ecuadorian rain forest for oil exploration. The Chinese are mining lithium in Chile, buying Brazilian beef and iron ore, and running up the price of American real estate by buying prime properties for cash.

The Chinese economic assault recently hit home with us. Our May reservations for 30 family members at Little Dix Bay have been canceled because—we are told—a Chinese syndicate has bought that 5-star former Rockresort and is closing it for 18 months for "renovation"(!). Mind you, Little Dix bay is in the British Virgin Islands.

But the invasion goes both ways. While the Chinese invest vast sums of American dollars in the Western Hemisphere, the Chinese population is being altered—should we say infected—by a cultural invasion from America. While billions of U.S. dollars flow to China for the manufacture of products at non-union labor rates (cheap labor being China's number one resource), billions of Chinese Yuan flow back to the U.S. for Apple iPhones, Boeing jets, Ford automobiles, Pizza Hut pizza, KFC chicken, and American movies. And, in the process, the cross cultivation of cheesy American movies, music, and social media must be driving the Chinese overlords crazy as the Chinese social order frays and the population threatens American style disorder.

Because we are the world's two leading economic powers, we are intertwined and codependent in huge areas. And because of the unalterable effect of the Internet and wide open travel opportunities, neither giant can stem the influence—either the economic or the cultural assault—of the other. It's an inevitable and unalterable marriage of two radically diverse cultures. And, like any marriage of opposites, it's bound to have its problems.

And in this case divorce isn't an option.

2/8/16

Ciao, Jovial, Iconic Mossback

ANTONIN SCALIA IS BEING lionized as a great American and a great legal scholar. I will happily write a spirited dissent on both scores. I have a strong suspicion that those who cast him as a great American have never read some of his opinions in criminal law, usually dissents, and those who rank him as a great constitutional lawyer have never studied the Constitutional provisions he relied on, or the history of the Constitutional Convention in Colonial America.

Because Scalia was always considered to be brilliant and scholarly, his pronouncements were taken at face value on faith, particularly by the political right wing. Only law school professors, Colonial America historians, and fellow Supreme Court members have had the standing and the temerity to challenge his reliably vehement opinions on law and morality. But now that he's dead and the eulogizing is coming to a close, objective historians can test the validity of his dogma in the fields of criminal law and civil liberties and public health.

Scalia claimed he was a strict constructionist when it came to constitutional issues, but real legal scholars are now discovering that he ignored inconvenient words actually in the Constitutional text or added words himself to fit his interpretation of prose written 227 years ago in a far simpler era. The fact of the matter is that the framers of the U.S. Constitution could not foresee or even imagine the complexity of an electronic, technological society in the 21st century. Consequently all a 2016 SCOTUS member can do in resolving an issue never conceived of in 1789 is to summon up the context of the young American republic and try to divine how the 1789 draftsmen might view the issue and decide it.

But that's mostly constitutional law theory because, as my Constitutional Law Professor declared in 1952, what the Justices really do is decide on the current decision first, then gather the best historical and contextual reasons to support it. And how they decide on the question at hand obviously and unavoidably depends on their own personal background, philosophy, legal education, life experience, and even religious views.

The fact that the political and economic philosophy of a SCOTUS member actually comes into play in Supreme Court decisions is the reason that Court observers can almost always predict how the Court will vote in a given case, most often five to four because of the political party of the President who appointed each of the nine Justices.

It is now finally recognized that the Supreme Court is actually a third political arm of the U.S. government, with Justices appointed by Republican presidents voting one way and those appointed by Democratic presidents voting the other. Only once in awhile does a SCOTUS member cross the political divide so evident now in American politics. Earl Warren did it 50 years ago and was disparaged by Republican politicians. John Roberts did it on Obamacare and is now considered a renegade by the political Right.

Back to Scalia, the darling of the political Right Wing, the Tea Party, and the Catholic Church. It's no coincidence that he was appointed by a conservative President (Reagan) and that his decisions were 100 percent predictable. He voted against any proposal condemned by the Catholic Church. He voted "Republican" on any political issue, and pro-prosecution in any criminal case (he even voted against Miranda rights and against exoneration of a prisoner sentenced to death even if proof of innocence was offered). He claimed that the often-misquoted Second Amendment provided for individual gun ownership, and thus he totally ignored the "well-regulated militia" requirement in that provision.

The list could go on and on, but all the public

hears about Scalia is how jovial, jolly, and fun-loving he was—jokes, opera, parties, charisma—but not how he voted in specific cases. Only legal scholars will, in time, be able to dim his aura.

If there was any doubt left about the fact that a SCOTUS member is really a political animal, the hullabaloo over whether President Obama will be allowed to appoint a replacement Justice—or should wait until a Republican is elected in November (?)—answers the question. This country has never been more polarized politically than it is in 2016, and that unfortunately encompasses the U.S. Supreme Court, which just lost a thoroughly partisan and predictable member.

2/20/16

Not Dumbfounded, but Maybe a Little Nervous

PEOPLE IN THE WORLD we live in are all dumb-founded, flabbergasted, baffled, and incredulous over the triumph of Donald Trump (historic name Drumpf), in the primaries thus far. They all ask the same question: How could such a blowhard buffoon and con man gather so much support that he is eclipsing Senators, Governors, a neurosurgeon, and Republican stalwarts? They can't believe what has happened in this campaign and they never stop talking about it.

I'm surprised, but far from dumbfounded. Surprised that Trump hasn't made enough blunders to start fading away in the polls. But not surprised over the fact that millions of Americas, mostly elderly, white, blue collar, and red neck, have responded favorably to Trump's rabble rousing rants and tirades. The reason I'm neither shocked nor surprised is that I was once a young soldier in the United States Army, probably alive today because of my 1927 birth date and the two atomic bombs; I missed the combat because I was only 17 in 1944 and 18 in 1945, and because we were training in Texas for the ultimate invasion of Honshu when the bombs ended WWII in August, 1945.

I learned at age 18, in Texas and Korea, that there was a huge slice of the American public that I never knew existed while sheltered in a California private school, then at Stanford and Oregon State Universities. It was made up of young white males from Texas, Arkansas, Oklahoma, Tennessee, Kentucky, Georgia, and the Gulf States—raw, rustic, ribald, and uncouth young males with little or no college education. They were now away from their bucolic home environment for the first time. They were in an army that had won the war, vanquished both Germany and Japan, and was now literally in charge of the world.

You can probably imagine how these proud young rustics treated the Koreans and Japanese population that we were occupying in 1946. I was so disgusted about the way our GI's often abused the "gooks" in Korea that I wrote a letter expressing my dismay to *TIME* magazine and they published it. (Knowing me, wouldn't you think I would have kept a copy.)

Those young rubes from the South and Middle America are now in their eighties, if alive, and they are the matrix of the millions who now support a blowhard buffoon who is smart enough to trade on their fears and frustrations by touting strength, power, easy solutions, and suspicion of the so-called "Establishment."

The American rubes don't have enough intellect to look past the bluster and bloviating for a plan, anything feasible or having a prayer in a dysfunctional Congress. They operate at a level of primitive emotion—fear, anger, frustration, and bravado.

While Trump could conceivably capture enough delegates to claim the nomination, or at least force a third party, I can't see how he could win the general election, despite the large number of red states in the South and mid-America. Both coasts are blue, the West Coast completely and the East Coast to Virginia, and that's where a lot of educated people live who think that Trump is now an unfunny joke. If the Republican party management can't succeed in offloading Donald by July, I think the brighter, or saner, half of the American electorate will do so in November.

But this is how German intellectuals and professionals were regarding a house painter named Adolf Hitler in 1937 and 1938 and 1939. And look what happened there when a clever blowhard rabble-rouser outwitted, then terrified, the kinder, gentler, saner segments of the German population.

Hopefully a healthy corps of investigative journalists and an unblinking, unyielding array of media in 2016 U.S. will bring down this baffling, disturbing, crafty con man.

3/1/16

What Language Will The Millennials Speak?

THE ENGLISH LANGUAGE HAS by far the most extensive vocabulary, with approximately 172,000 basic words in the Oxford English Dictionary and many more thousands of variations. More words are added daily and thousands of French, Latin, and German words are part of our professional vocabulary.

English is the international standard, even though it is the native tongue of only 5 percent or 6 percent of the globe's 7 ½ billion people. It has been a major topic in British and American Universities for ages and the average higher-educated American has a vocabulary between 20,000 and 80,000 words.

But that skill is rapidly changing and in the wrong direction. American test compilers have decided that the teenage vocabulary is shrinking to the point where words previously on the SAT and other aptitude tests have now been eliminated in favor of words in daily use and more essay time. If you saw the words they decided to eliminate, you would agree with my thesis—that the Millennials are clearly going to have a smaller vocabulary in English than we have. Words not in common or daily use will become obsolete except in literature by pre-Millennial authors. They may even be described as "obsolete" in the 2020 dictionary.

So the two questions are, Why is this happening and What's the difference if it is? The answer to the first question lies in the works of Shakespeare, Maughm, Shaw, and Edwin Newman. The answer is that they had big enough vocabularies and enough literacy to use the right word for the right context. Synonyms may or may not fit to simplify something complex or nuanced.

Edwin Newman celebrated language as an exact science, not an approximation. And it was Mark Twain who said that the difference between the right word and the almost-right word is the difference between lightning and a lightning bug. Serious or complex expression, especially written, may require words no longer known to the next generation because they aren't learning them in English classes or in English Literature.

How many of your grandkids read British or American novels written before 1940? How many could pass the Stanford Aptitude Test on vocabulary? And how many know the difference between lie and lay, or fewer and less, or it's and its? And have you seen anything in teen texts that a 12 year old wouldn't understand?

I don't expect my grandkids and great grandkids (now 12 of them…) to be semanticists, literary lions, or academic researchers. But I hope they progress far deeper into our mother tongue than their cohorts do in teenage texting and social prattle, because it isn't enough just to exist and adjust and observe. It's just as important in the long run, at least for some of us, to define and delineate and inscribe. And to do so with enough precision to be satisfying.

Insidious means more than sneaky. Invidious means more than bad. Obsequious means more than kissy. Stultify means more than embarrass. And lassitude means more than tired.

There's no one-word synonym for crepuscular. Or avuncular. Or manqué. Or trepidation. Or pontificate. Or bloviate.

So why not use the right word instead of a lot of near misses? But you can't do that unless you've read a lot of serious literature. Or studied vocabulary as an assignment, as many of us did 70 or 75 years ago … so long ago that I've forgotten some of the $2 words I learned at The Academy and Stanford.

3/31/16

Benevolence on Steroids: When Do-Gooders and Yentas Spawn Tyranny

We're WELL SUPPLIED WITH stories of child abuse, domestic violence, and drunk driving. Law enforcement agencies are well-tuned and ready to roll when concerned, public-spirited citizens call to report a problem.

But what you don't often hear about are cases where dedicated do-gooders—or dedicated personal enemies—call to report an offense of some kind, an unattended child in a car, or on the street, a violation of Homeowners Association rules, a noisy domestic squabble, an erratic driver, an agitated or over-active vagrant, or a passenger speaking Arabic.

There are two trends at work that increase the number of citizen calls to report an offense. The first is the arrival, about twenty years ago, of terrorists and terrorism as a new menace. Because terrorists strike without warning and can be supremely destructive, public surveillance and public suspicion have been enlisted by government itself as the first line of defense against our countless unseen enemies at home and abroad.

It's now an unofficial public duty to observe and report any strange or unusual activity. Because of the history of Islamic terrorism, a certain amount of cultural and racial profiling is inherently involved. We have actually developed a silent strain of cultural paranoia or xenophobia because our enemies are unseen, lethal, and tend to be foreign.

The World Trade Center attack, the Fort Hood Massacre, the failed airline shoe bomb, the Boston Marathon bombing, and the San Bernardino massacre have millions of Americans on unofficial alert for more terrorist attacks by Islamic enemies (Thank you again, Bush and Cheney, for destroying Iraq.)

If you think the terrorism-alert paranoia is bad today, just hope we don't produce a flock of domestic suicide bombers who could wreak havoc in stadiums, arenas, terminals, or even public gatherings. Or home grown monsters who can easily acquire shoulder-fired rocket launchers and bring down jet aircraft in landing or takeoff patterns completely outside airports.

When it comes to citizens reporting suspicious activity, I can't help but remember Nazi Germany 75 years ago, where neighbors, and even family members, were encouraged to report any sign of disaffection to the Gestapo. If the U.S. approaches that level of civil surveillance, the Islamic terrorists will have already won.

But the second pressure on law enforcement agencies is far more subtle and has nothing to do with foreign or Islamic threats. It's the rise of home-grown moral and civil imperatives spawned by religious crusaders, racial and political activists, and hare-brained politicians and administrators who bow to the will of the loudest or best organized activists for a given cause. I would call it benevolence or do-goodism on steroids, and it thrives in a so-called democracy where the loudest free speech may prevail—and squelch less attractive free speech.

I'm thinking of the craven "political correctness" movement in literature and politics, and the "Don't Offend" campaigns on college campuses. While the do-gooders and angry minority activists are campaigning to alter history and social science, and even true science, on campus—and to change the faces on U.S. money and monuments in U.S. parks and mottos in government buildings—what they are really doing is abridging for their purposes the primary bedrock of democracy, namely, free speech.

What the legislators and college administrators and politicians forget during the ruckus is that the real strength of democracy lies in adversity, not conformity, and, as Walter Lippman observed long ago, "Where everyone thinks alike, no one thinks much."

Religious and social activists should have their

say, but not get their views codified in laws, ordinances, and Homeowners Ass'n rules. "Helicopter parents" may dominate PTA meetings, but shouldn't cause competent and caring "Free Range Parents" to have to spend vast sums on legal fees. Andrew Jackson and Woodrow Wilson may have held views not popular with today's moralists, but they are legitimate figures in U.S. history. And history and science should be exempt from alteration to conform to today's ethos and mores, or it would no longer be history and science.

Ironically, one reason the Republican buffoon is so incomprehensibly popular is that he throws political correctness and social decorum to the wind. More power to him there, but unfortunately all that does is reveal his basic boorishness and vacuousness.

All I would say to the dedicated do-gooders and social activists is congratulations on your dedication and good intentions, but do remember that the road to hell is paved with good intentions.

4/26/16

A Worthy but Hopeless Quest:
Re-Stocking Our Corps of Journalists

IF I WERE EMPEROR of the Civilized World, I would try to solve a growing and deadly imbalance in two critical occupational categories that provide oversight and exposure of our troubled society. Both groups monitor and scrutinize our governmental and corporate activity, both public and back room. Both groups profit through exposure of a seemingly endless streak of corruption and malfeasance in our governmental and corporate chambers. Such is the heritage of human nature operating in a relatively "free society," a democracy. And without both groups, corruption and betrayal would run rampant, as it does in third world nations that don't have these two corps of watchdogs and exposers.

In the past 50 or 60 years, the first group, the legal profession, has increased by leaps and bounds. Because of a Twentieth-Century notion that lawyers make loads of money and have superior political power, which, in the last fifty years, spawned a spate of private, for-profit law schools, the number of graduating law students has vastly exceeded the market for new attorneys, and there is a surplus of American lawyers. One joke in recent years is that there is a special line for attorneys in the Unemployment Office.

The other group of society's watchdogs is much smaller and has been shrinking rapidly in the Internet era. I'm referring to journalists, and most particularly investigative journalists. I don't know how many universities even have a School of Journalism any more, but I'm sure the number is shrinking—and so is the number of students even considering journalism as a profession. It has never been a glamorous profession, or one offering the potential bonanza or political traction of law ... and the whole field of journalism is dying as both magazines and newspapers close their doors and the public does its reading on the Internet, if at all. (The same decline is rampant in book publishing and bookstore sales).

For 42 years on *Sixty Minutes*, Mike Wallace was an icon investigative journalist. Morley Safer is now retiring after 46 years on the same program. Who is going to replace Mike Wallace and Morley Safer —and Carl Bernstein and Bob Woodward of the *Washington Post* (Watergate)? Who is going to roam the corridors in Washington, D.C. or root out the whistle-blowers in government and corporate ranks?

In fact, who will a whistle-blower even spill to if he wants a bright light to shine on betrayal or a risk to public safety?

Good luck getting our overworked and understaffed FBI agents, DJ attorneys, and prosecuting attorneys to uncover the next Watergate, or Bridgegate, or Inflategate, or Takatagate. They all have full dockets and no time to go fishing for more dirt.

A few publications still probe and question government and corporate activity, but with very limited budgets and readership. We get *Progressive, In These Times, The Washington Spectator,* Jim Hightower's *Lowdown, TIME,* and *The Week,* among others. And there is definitely some first rate investigative journalism in *Frontline* and *Sixty Minutes* and the network news programs. But I worry about the scope and future of investigative journalism and wish there was some way to divert some of the legions of law school hopefuls to whatever journalism schools still exist—and to offer them some prestigious outlets for their work once they graduate.

But it's probably a hopeless pursuit, like the quest for a functioning Congress, a politics-free Supreme Court, and a widely-admired U.S. President.

5/12/16

An Ideal Pit Crew for
the Long Race

A S YOU RUN PAST your life expectancy by a decade or two or, in my case, three, you find that you need a far different pit crew than you did as a youth. Your support group then was obviously family, close relatives, pals, and teachers. In middle age it becomes your partner, fellow employees, and your closest friends. But if you live long enough, the cast of important characters in your life changes radically through attrition, through deterioration, and through reorientation. In short, through survival and through experience.

When I was born in 1927, the year Lindbergh made it to Paris, the life expectancy for a white U.S. male was probably in the low 60s. It was many decades later when it got into the high 60s and 8 decades later before it got into the mid-70s (depending on state of residence). I'm already a couple of decades past my 1927 life expectancy and plan to exceed it by three.

Longevity has its advantages, but it comes with some serious costs. My grandparents departed first, long ago. Then my parents and almost all of my high school and law school classmates, decades ago. Then virtually all of my tennis, racquetball, and travel pals, leaving widows to have periodic gal pal luncheons.

All my aunts and uncles died decades ago and my few surviving cousins are in their 80s and 90s, none out here in the West.

Since I had no siblings there were never in-laws or nieces and nephews. And the fact that I closed my office and sold the building 20 years ago, then we basically abandoned the Presbyterian Church and the Tennis Club, gives you a picture that might sound forlorn to the average person, lonely and abandoned.

But fortunately that's not the case for me, or for Maralys either. As an "only" and a "Navy brat"—lots of moving around—I have always been comfortable in my own company, and never became a joiner or party animal. I miss the tennis and the skiing and the trips with pals more than I miss the pals. A reasonable schedule of concerts and family trips and discussion group sessions is all the social life I need.

Maralys, on the other hand, being a much more social animal, enjoys her class, her critique group, and her gal-pal luncheons or theater dates as adjuncts to our joint calendar, so we both feel adequately "booked."

What inspired this piece is a declaration I recently

made to my dentist. Seeing him three times in a period of four weeks led me to realize that the pit crew I will need for my golden oldie 90s will consist of three people who become more important every year—my marital partner, my dentist, and my orthopedic surgeon.

In the middle years we take our marital partner for granted, in my case too much so. But serious old age brings an increased level of fragility and feebleness that makes a caregiver partnership ever more important. Eldercare homes are full of seniors who lost or never had a marital partner, and who can afford the care. The physical and emotional dependency of marital senility is something those in healthy, confident middle age would never anticipate. Far better to face unexpected but inevitable emotional and physical shocks as a pair than as a lone senior.

Then there's the orthopedic surgeon who'd better be standing by your side in your 80s and 90s, particularly if you inherited strong osteoarthritis genes. I got them from both sides and now know why both parents froze up and suffered in their 80s and 90s. Those genes, plus two decades of overweight and a ski accident, led me to ten orthopedic surgeries in the last 20 years. Even without the OA genes and a corporate lifestyle, I doubt that my knees and hips and shoulders would have made it to 89 without some spare parts.

And even Maralys, at 87, without serious OA genes, has two artificial knees, reorganized metatarsals, a repaired right shoulder, and corticosteroid injections every three months for arthritic pain here and there. In fact, any senior approaching the 90s with original hips, knees, shoulders, and spine is a rare bird and probably still needs an orthopedic surgeon on call.

That brings me to my dentist. I should probably have Big Bob Meckstreth on speed dial because I still have all of my original teeth —28 minus the wisdoms— despite the fact that my family owned a Karmelkorn shop when I was a kid and I've had a love affair with milk shakes, colas, and chocolate for almost 80 years. I've had so much gold in my mouth since my college and Army years that I looked like a Filipino Colonel when I smiled, but thanks to at least five good dentists from Honolulu to Westwood to Santa Ana, I still have at least the roots of 28 teeth.

But parts keep falling off, no thanks to Tracy for the licorice toffee, so I finally told Dr. Meckstroth that he had better be on call during my Nineties. And thanked him for doing a sudden root canal on #13 so I could enjoy our family powwow on Virgin Gorda, British Virgin Islands last month.

6/14/16

Well, You Love Your Pet, Don't You?

THIS IS A QUESTION many a vet asks a pet owner, either overtly or tacitly. The question, and the answer, comes on the heels of a disturbing diagnosis, a plan of action, and a recitation of the fees involved. It's a challenge most of the tens of millions of American pet owners never have to deal with, but one that literally millions of others do.

The incredible number of dog and cat owners in the U.S. has spawned a huge and profitable pet service and supply industry, with revenue reported in the billions of dollars. For example, two of the largest vendors of pet supplies and equipment, PetSmart and Petco have revenue reported as seven billion dollars and one billion dollars a couple of years ago, before being snapped up by private investors. And those figures don't cover the countless smaller, local firms that board, launder, shampoo, primp, pamper, manicure and exercise pets, primarily dogs.

But the big money flows, and the biggest shocks for pet owners come, in veterinary clinics and veterinary hospitals. Most of these thousands of institutions are privately owned and not affiliated, so revenue is not publicly available. But any pet owner whose pet develops an unusual problem, for example a pelvic fracture, or viral corneal infection, or a severe distemper, will quickly learn how expensive veterinary medicine has become.

Probably because the fees charged in veterinary medicine are not regulated by any governmental agency, and because pet owners become so attached to their furry friends that they cannot refuse even outrageously inflated charges, many charges for pet surgery or specialized care far exceed similar care for humans.

Our son, an orthopedic surgeon, cites examples of almost comical disparity between human and animal surgical fees; for example, a surgeon's standard fee for a total hip, is somewhere less than $2,000, whereas a total hip on a dog or cat can run $5,000 or more.

The cruel fact is that a veterinary surgeon can charge "whatever the traffic will bear," meaning how much an adoring pet owner can afford, or the pet insurance company will pay ... whereas both the Federal Government and the major medical insurance companies have set limits on what an orthopedic, thoracic, general, or neurological surgeon can charge.

We've owned a number of cats over the years, but until this year we've never had occasion to learn the harsh bite of veterinary medicine. I never thought I would spend four figures on a cat, but Pretty Boy was very special and a close "personal friend" for seven years, so I surprised even myself by spending almost $5,000 in a hopeless effort to reverse his renal failure.

But recently we learned again how vets are quietly gathering a lot of gold simply because they can. A month ago we accepted a replacement for Pretty Boy, and in three weeks had over $500 invested in initial vet care ... when, after two exams, our kindly vet said she didn't like "Smarty Pants" left eye, so she referred us to a veterinary clinic specializing in dog and cat eyes ... yes, just eyes.

The first surprise was the size and activity level of the animal eye clinic. The place was a beehive of pet owners with dogs and cats being seen in six exam rooms by four vets who specialize in animal eyes ... Then the shock came after the $181 exam of Smarty Pants' eye. The vet exam took about ten minutes (with a slit lamp), then the discussion of the appropriate surgery and treatment took about fifteen minutes with a sweet clinic tech.

It turned out that Smarty Pants needs a corneal graft because of a viral, non-treatable lesion on the left cornea, cause and source unknown ("maybe from the mother"). Surgery and post-op would run a hair under

$3,000, payable in advance. Aftercare would last one year and would involve lots of eye meds and a neck cone.

Long story short. We informed the sweet tech that, at 89 and 87, with a few things going on in our lives, that wasn't a plan we could live with. I asked if someone involved with the clinic could take over Smarty Pants and handle the surgery and aftercare. Amazingly and fortuitously, Shannon said that she does place cats and had six fourteen-week-old kittens at home ... I sadly signed off ownership of Smarty Pants and we went home with an empty cat carrier and a sense of amazed relief.

We are now looking for a veterinary clinic to invest in—and maybe or maybe not another cat.

6/22/16

A Deviation Celebration:
How About Giving It a Rest?

Let me be the first to say enough gay pride already. Take your rainbow flags out of my face, stop chanting and marching, and go quietly home to your now-legally-protected "alternative lifestyle". Go on with your life and keep your sex life, whatever it is, nice and private.

At discussion group recently I compared the dichotomous eras in our sexual history, the first several thousand years when homosexuality was considered a "crime against nature" and punished as "sodomy", then the dawn of homosexual liberation maybe fifty years ago, to now, when the theme is "Proud to Be Gay" and the LGBT campaign is loud and ubiquitous. The White House and national monuments are swathed in rainbow colors, the media are swamped with gay celebration, especially since Orlando, and Gay Pride parades seem to spring up everywhere.

I reminded the group why Oscar Wilde and Peter Tchaikovsky never wore "Proud To Be Gay" tee shirts. Oscar Fingal O'Flahertie WILLS Wilde died a broken 46-year-old on the Continent after serving two years at hard labor in England following a "sodomy" conviction. And Tchaikovsky committed suicide by taking arsenic to mimic death by cholera (the "official" cause of death), so that a formal letter confirming his homosexuality would not be delivered to the Czar.

Until fifty years ago, no one knew how many homosexuals there were in society, except their therapists, because they all stayed "in the closet." And transgender surgery wasn't an option or discussed.

Now no form of " alternative lifestyle" sexual conduct is condemned except bestiality and pedophilia—I haven't seen any of those weirdos in parades—so the millions recently out of the closet now seem compelled to tout their lifestyle as some sort of special attribute, something to be proud of and to celebrate. Well I say, fine, go lead your deviant lives in peace and thank you for not adding to the population bomb. Just stop waving that pretty flag in my face, stop chanting, and don't look for me to get a "Proud To Be Hetero" tee shirt.

6/28/16

P.S. Twenty years ago I tried a female-to-male transgender case against my client, a plastic surgeon. We prevailed over the very strange patient and I remember

Judge Jerald Oliver taking me into chambers and asking, "How does he/she pee?"

RVW

"The Ugly American" Gets a Whole New Meaning.

WHENEVER YOU RUN INTO a person who favors Trump, what do you do? Unless they quickly indicate it's a joke and they're just pulling our leg, we quickly conclude that we have either a yahoo or an unbalanced, quirky individual on our hands.

If it's a yahoo, we know that Trump has natural appeal because of his simplistic views and his boorishness. But if it's an educated or otherwise formidable man or woman, we simply scratch our heads and wonder if they are simply out of touch with the outside world, media shy, or seriously disturbed about the shape, color, and direction of American society.

If that's the case, I can understand a lament that the America I grew up in 75 years ago is gone and not coming back—in nostalgia we remember only the good stuff and our youth. But to accept a blowhard, snarky buffoon like Trump as a solution to our social and economic turmoil defies all reason.

The only suggestion I have for any literate Trump fan is to read the article in the current New Yorker magazine about Trump's ghostwriter for his famous book, *The Art of The Deal,* thirty years ago. It turns out that Tony Schwartz was the actual author of the book and he found it impossible to get Trump to focus on anything for more than a few minutes so, with Trump's consent, he gathered a lot of his material by phone-tapping Donald's phone conversations and tapping his associates and family.

The Art of The Deal made millions and Schwartz got rich because he had settled for 50 percent of the advance and royalties. He is therefore currently somewhat guilt-ridden about telling the truth about Donald Trump. But he says that if he wrote the book today he would entitle it *The Sociopath,* and he feels that the American electorate needs to know the truth about a big phony—or we are headed for an extremely dangerous election.

WE couldn't agree more.

7/27/16

"This Is my Country"???

THIS MORNING FOR SOME reason I recalled the words of a WWII era patriotic song called "This is My Country." Proud and triumphant, the words proclaimed, "This is my country, land of my birth. This is my country, grandest on earth. I pledge thee my allegiance, America the bold, Yes, this is my country, to have and to hold".

Can you imagine such a proud paean today? Not likely. In a country torn apart by racial and social strife, a country whose legislature is so polarized that the two parties hardly speak and get almost nothing done, and a country where, in six weeks, a boorish, unhinged redneck may get thirty or forty million votes for Leader of The World, it's a little difficult to wave the flag and celebrate our superiority.

Our illustrious nation has a huge military budget that obscures all others, yet we've lost four wars and won zero in seventy one years. A nation that produced *Oklahoma, Show Boat, The King and I, My Fair Lady,* and *Paint Your Wagon* now celebrates a frenetic combo of rap and calisthenics as the most successful Broadway show in decades. The Fourth Estate thrives on incompetence in government (the VA, Flint, FEMA, FDA) and corruption in the corporate suites (Wells Fargo, Mylan, Countrywide, ad nauseum).

So the question is whether patriotism is in temporary hibernation or whether it is permanently replaced by disaffection and cynicism.

Perhaps our problem is too much information in a totally wired world. We read too much non-fiction and watch only informational TV. We avoid talk radio like a disease and see few of the rare "adult" movies. We share perspective with foreign friends who wonder what "happened to" the U.S.? My last contact with yahoos and rustics was 70 years ago in the U.S. Army. Maralys has never even been near them in her extended cocoon.

Good luck to the next U.S. President. The country is a mess, socially, politically, legally (even the SCOTUS), and physically (aging infrastructure is on the edge). And God help us all if Hilary stumbles, the yahoos storm the polls, the minorities whine but don't vote, and Donald Trumpelthinskin gets the nuclear button.

9/23/17

Only In America: A Colony Of Doomsday Minutemen

For those of you who don't read *THE WEEK* from cover to cover, I have a news flash for you. I haven't seen or heard of it in other news media, but it lines up perfectly with everything else that is occurring in 2016 America.

It involves what I would call redneck Libertarians, Survivalists, Militiamen, "Freedom Fighters," "Sovereigns," and sundry anti-government malcontents who see Armageddon or social collapse on the horizon. They see it coming from any of several sources—nuclear, political, or economic, all stemming from a tyrannical but weak U.S. government. They are basically retreating from Democrat-controlled urban America to an area far from U.S. cities and populated by other dissidents who share their paranoia and ultra-conservative politics.

The movement and the area is known as the American Redoubt, a term I never heard before today.

It seems to be centered on the area around Hayden and Coeur D'Alene in northern Idaho, with some extension into lightly populated areas of Western Montana, Eastern Washington, and Eastern Oregon. The area was apparently chosen by early survivalists because of remoteness from seats of government, availability of acreage at affordable prices, and the sylvan environment.

The Redoubt population apparently numbers in the low thousands. They are exclusively Caucasian, ultraconservative in politics, "God-fearing" pioneers who store large quantities of food and ammunition in what sound like bunkers. (The word "redoubt" means stronghold in old English). Local government has "a light regulatory touch and friendly gun laws."

Apparently the movement is growing enough to be purchasing water purifiers, solar panels, hand-cranked radios, $3,000 portable freeze dryers (900 per month), and blast-proof underground steel bunkers, which sell for up to $150,000.

In other words, these are people who soured on modern society, see doom on the horizon, and are hunkering down in fortresses built in a pristine environment with funds derived from assets accumulated in urban America.

There are enough of them to have created a real estate broker called Revolutionary Realty and a radio station called Prepper Broadcasting. As you might expect, many of the Redoubt clan are former police, firefighters, and military who would vote for Trump and think Hillary would be a "disaster." They regard themselves as God-fearing, Christian, freedom-fighting conservatives who have a live-and-let-live ethos.

Like the Quakers, Amish, and Mormon fundamentalists, these people have retreated from what they feel is a corrupt, intrusive, and dangerous society. They are moving backwards and away from the leading edge. Rather than to try to help solve our urban and political mess, they abandon it and adopt primitive skills and military protection.

So I guess the question is, are they just quitters and deserters? Are they prescient survivalists? Or are they simply yahoos who rusticated? Or maybe a combination of all three.

10/9/16

Just What We Need:
More Impaired Drivers

CALIFORNIA IS ABOUT TO add another problem for law enforcement and highway safety. If Proposition 64 passes, as expected, the County Jail population may ease off for awhile, though not nearly as significantly as the pot lobby claims because most arrests these days involve methamphetamine and drugs a lot more exotic than marijuana. Arrests for possession of the quantities of marijuana allowed by Prop 64 are NOT the problem today.

But your safety in a car will be reduced more than the pot proponents would ever admit. Washington legalized marijuana in 2012. An Auto Club Foundation has now reported that one in six Washington drivers involved in fatal crashes tested positive for THC (the impairing pot ingredient). Before legalization the THC percentage was only one in 12. Because of current problems in relating THC blood levels to impairment,

Washington created statutory "per se" limits of THC for law enforcement purposes. California may have to do the same because there is no breathalyzer technology as yet for THC impairment.

The National Highway Traffic Safety Administration reported that the number of weekend nighttime drivers with THC in their system rose 50 percent nationally from 2007 to 2014, no doubt aided by marijuana being legal in 5 U.S. jurisdictions. Making it legal in California will only increase the numbers.

The singsong response to legalization opposition has always been, well, everyone is using it already, so why not make it legal and empty the prisons? The answer is that the prisons will still be full—of meth, heroin, cocaine, and exotic drug users, not to mention myriad personal and property crimes. And there is a certain percentage of the population, even in 2016, that avoids breaking the law, but will finally join the party and start smoking pot "like everyone else".

So add some of them to the drivers out there who are a little high on THC, and then hope the CHP sends a few officers for DRE training. This is a program run by the International Association of Chiefs of Police, with the encouragement of the NHTSA. Because there is no breathalyzer or field sobriety test for THC impairment, and different individuals have different levels of impairment, Drug Recognition Experts are specially trained to deal with THC impaired driving.

The bad news is that there are only 8400 DRE's nationwide—out of 1.1 million police officers. So, typical of a democracy, the populace adopts a neato program, then waits for the legislature to deal with the side effects and collateral damage later.

It's bad enough now, with alcohol-fueled drivers under the influence. So let's add a couple hundred thousand more driving under the influence of THC— but thinking they're doing just fine, just fine. Just fine.

So drive extra carefully after November 8.

10/27/16

A "Reasonable Time"
Doesn't Mean Never

M Y SPECIALTY IN LAW school was constitutional law and my interest in it helped me win the State moot court championship (oral argument) in 1953. So I'm a little baffled by what is going on in thoroughly-dysfunctional Washington, D.C.

I think the Federal Administration has some legal room to sue the Republican leader(s) of the Senate for flagrant violation of Article II, Section II of the U.S. Constitution, causing serious legal damage to the Republic.

The lawsuit should be framed as a mandamus action to force the leaders of the Senate to hold a hearing to review the nomination of a new member of the U.S. Supreme Court. Antonin Scalia died on February 13, 2016, leaving a vacancy on the most important governmental body in Washington. President Obama nominated Merrick Garland, a highly-respected Judge, to fill the vacancy on March 16, 2016, almost 8 months ago.

The Republican-controlled Senate has first refused to hold a hearing before the November 8 Federal election, in the hopes a Republican would win and make an appointment more to their liking. Now, some Republican Senators, led by John McCain of Arizona, are threatening to hold no confirmation hearing for four years if Hillary Clinton wins on November 8. In other words, the Republicans are refusing to conform to the express language of Article II, Section II, which reads:

"The President ... shall nominate and by and with the Advice and Consent of the Senate, shall appoint ... Judges of the Supreme Court and all other Officers of the United States, whose Appointments are not herein otherwise provided for and which shall be established by Law."

The Republicans seem to feel that they are under no duty to render "Advice and Consent" on a nomination because the Constitution specifies no timetable or deadline for a hearing. But a good Constitutional Law lawyer would respond to that argument rather sharply with a reminder that the Constitution draftsmen were not simpletons and they assumed that their successors who had to enforce it would likewise not be nincompoops.

Before 1789, and endless times since, lawyers,

leaders, and other arbiters of rules and regulations have had to fill in a lot of blanks with logic and educated inference. The word "reasonable" is used frequently in cases where a predecessor author or draftsman failed to specify details for executing a policy or mandate. For example, innumerable legal cases turn on what the fictitious "reasonable and prudent man" would do under the circumstances. Conduct appropriate for "a reasonable and prudent man" is whatever a judge or jury decides it is. And an action required to be taken without a specified timetable or deadline would in most cases be decided to be "within a reasonable time," another oft-used, handy legal standard.

Therefore I assume a good constitutional law expert should be able to persuade a Federal Judge, a Federal Appellate Court, or the U.S. Supreme Court itself that the framers of the Constitution would never have specified the "Advice and Consent" of the Senate if it was never to occur. Failing to specify a deadline or timetable, they clearly intended that action to take place "within a reasonable time." And I would argue that "a reasonable time" would mean before a given Senate session terminates.

So Attorney General Loretta Lynch, and more specifically U.S. Solicitor General Ian Gershengorn, get to work.

11/2/16

WE ARE IN SHOCK

WE ARE IN SHOCK, along with the West Coast and the educated portion of the East Coast (Virginia northward), partly because we were all misled by the pollsters and political talking heads, and partly because this country now has a narcissistic carnival barker as President.

I am a little less shocked than the rest of our clan because I was in the U.S. army three generations ago and found out that there really are two Americas, with intellectuals on the Coasts and lots of yahoos in the middle.

The Redneck Revolution of 2016 represents a rejection of U.S. demographic and social change of the last thirty or forty years. Donald the huckster promised, in disguised terms, a return to the good old-fashioned white (Northern European) America I grew up in before World War II, when America was protected by two great oceans and Boy Scout morality within. As

121

his fans will soon find out, that America is dead and gone, and cannot be revived.

The world has shrunk. America has been invaded. The demographics are changed, in both color and volatility. And, thanks to that Constitution the Republicans hold so dear, Donald Trump will be almost powerless to change the face and security of 2016 U.S.

Last night I told Lauren that the sun would still rise and shine today, despite America's latest blunder. We ourselves have lost 2 ½ sons, survived the Depression, WWII, and 65 years of nuclear weapons at the ready, and we will never be poor or without good medical care, so I refuse to let shock progress to depression, because I know that Trump will undoubtedly be a big, dumb mistake by non-intellectual Americans, but he will quickly learn the limitations on his power, and hopefully stay away from the nuclear button.

So I suggest that everyone take a deep breath and read the first three Articles of the Constitution, just as Trump will be forced to do ... We have survived bigger threats than this, and so has America, although I don't think we've ever had such an unqualified executive (even Andrew Jackson?). In such a precarious time, it reminds me of an old sick joke. "Hire the handicapped—they're fun to watch."

11/9/16

AN OBSOLETE SYSTEM IN A CREAKY CONSTITUTION

CAN YOU THINK OF anything that's 200 years old and still works well? Not much chance in a rapidly changing world. Time changes everything. Revision and remodeling are unavoidable.

So is it any wonder that there is so much discussion about the antiquated electoral college system spelled out in Article II, Section 1 of a document drafted 227 years ago in a rudimentary society after weeks of bitter debate?

What people observe is that this concocted system doesn't always reflect the popular vote—missing it this time by well over one million votes—but what most don't know is what inspired the electoral college device in 1787. If they did know, the screams for abolition would be much louder than they are today.

Probably the biggest issue in the final Constitution debate—the deal breaker—was slavery. The slave owners were located in the Southern States, but the heavier population was in the Northern States. The Southern State representatives not only vetoed abolition of slavery in the Constitution, but they got Negroes counted as 2/3 of a person for population purposes—without a vote—and they concocted the electoral college system to make sure that the Northern States couldn't vote out slavery (setting the stage for a war 74 years later).

The math was a little complex, but every state got two Senators, regardless of population, and the net effect was to protect the slave owners for over 70 years. And even today the Presidential vote still doesn't reflect the actual U.S. population accurately.

The electoral college is only one area in which our hallowed Constitution is rickety and totally out of sync with 2016 America. Appointing Supreme Court Justices for life meant 10 or 15 years in 1787. Today it could mean up to 50 or even 60 years (there is no minimum age limit). And since we no longer have citizen "militias" as they conceived them in 1789, the language of the very brief Second Amendment in no way says what the NRA and some of the Supremes say it says.

So when you hear a politician—or a SCOTUS nominee—say that he is a "strict constructionist," you are listening to either a phony or someone unschooled in constitutional law or political history.

11/18/16

DECEMBER, 2016

NOW THAT THE DISGUSTING election is over, and we have a boorish, unhinged amateur slated for inauguration in seven weeks, we would be wise to try to ignore Trump, Pence, and the redneck revolution for awhile. But it's going to be very hard to do because the press and TV are completely fascinated by this blowhard loose cannon—and his early choices for the Cabinet and SCOTUS promise nothing but endless scandals, fiascos, and controversy for much of 2017.

Maralys especially should avoid The Trump Tempest for awhile because her health has been affected by her obsession with the campaign and that one outrageous candidate. Currently she has several systems under treatment, not necessarily because of The Donald.

Although I believed the polls and had faith in the ultimate good sense of the electorate—even the NASCAR segment of the electorate—Trump struck a nerve in angry red America, and also they couldn't stomach an articulate female attorney as President. So sixty two million angry, frustrated Americans put an egocentric sociopath in the White House. And the U.S. will probably never be the same country we were so proud of 70 years ago.

The reason I see nothing but controversy, unrest, and litigation in the next few years is because it's simply impossible to "Make America Great Again" by turning back the clock. I would be happy myself if we could do so, because I also remember a different America (although my two years in the U.S. Army did show me two Americas, not one). But the 340 million Americans in 2016 are a far different crowd than we had in the Nineteenth century, and they are so disparate (and spoiled by "big government") that they are going to be sullen, if not mutinous, under a Republican triad (both branches). Hillary would have had big problems, too.

So far what we have since November 8 is a lot of disgruntled or depressed friends and relations—but a higher stock market and a promise of greater infrastructure attention. What I hope to see from Donald and Paul Ryan is a huge back-pedaling in foreign aid and foreign military campaigns, plus a repatriation of several trillion dollars of overseas corporate earnings. And a decimation of the estate tax would be a nice gift to our next generation.

Turning to the overarching global crisis—one

that puts our election fiasco to shame—we see the climate change problem as only one reverberation of the population explosion. Every increase in the population, even in the Third World, increases the human footprint. The human footprint means deforestation (for crops or livestock) and generation of greenhouse gasses in numerous ways, like energy production, fuel consumption, manufacturing processes,and creature respiration.

So it will be impossible to attack problems of climate change, famine, water shortages, civil unrest, and mass immigration without trying to solve the underlying population explosion. And to address that problem you need two essentials—female education and free access to family planning systems.

Thus far the battle has been lost—thanks to the Catholic Church, a near-total lack of female education in the Third World countries, and the politics of the Republican party here in the U.S. (which has totally shut down family planning programs overseas by legislation and executive order, starting with George W. Bush's "Mexico City Rule" that he signed in 2001).

So far it sounds like Donald has been schooled by the anti-birth control stalwarts of the Republican Party, but there's no telling where that loose cannon is headed. In the meanwhile, I'm directing my charitable contributions to crusaders and educators like Population Connection, The Population Council, The Guttmacher Institute, and the Environmental Defense

Fund, rather than political or religious organizations. I encourage you to do the same. Because with 228,000 babies being born every day—far exceeding the death rate—and with the 7.4 billion humans headed for 10 billion by 2050, I'm very worried about the future for our 12 great grandchildren.

BUT the smartest way to live is to focus on the present, not the past or the future. And the photos show that we are still enjoying a bountiful life, both here and in the Virgin Islands and on Kauai. We were previously impressed by our ten grandkids, a handsome and productive lot. But now we are getting acquainted with their 12 kids, ages one to ten, and they seem to get smarter and better looking all the time.

After watching a clan of 37 on Virgin Gorda in May, with no accidents, disputes, or controversy, we knew we were lucky. And we still are.

So we will keep calm and carry on in 2017, chin up, chest forward, and spirits high. Or at least try. We hope you can do the same.

Journalists: to the Ramparts!

NOW THAT THE BALLOT box and Article II of the Constitution (the electoral college) have failed as lines of defense against stupidity and incompetency in the White House, our last line of defense will be the free press "guaranteed" by the First Amendment in 1789.

Once Trump is sworn in and his bizarre appointments cleared by a Republican Senate, there will be endless lawsuits in the Federal Courts. But the judiciary is somewhat reluctant to enter the political fray, and we have the fact that half of the Federal Judiciary, including the Supremes, was appointed by Reagan, Bush, and Bush since 1980. The litigation will take years and the judges will overturn only explicit violations of the Constitution or Federal laws. And even if they do, the Republican Congress can quickly remedy the problem by new legislation.

No, our only remaining real line of defense will consist of the "Fourth Estate" like never before, and

Trump, clearly demented but not stupid, has recognized that fact and declared war on what he calls "the crooked press." He will meet every challenge and exposè by the media with his usual vitriol and deprecation, and will clearly use all legal and economic power possible to silence his critics in the media.

The role of lawyers will be to persuade the courts—if not the Republican Congress—to preserve that last line of defense against tyranny and despotism, "freedom of the press" (with " free speech" the best words in the Constitution.) It's our bedrock U.S. political base, and if it fails, the U.S. we know is doomed, and probably the civilized world with it.

The other threat to the Fourth Estate is obviously the Internet, which has substantially diminished journalism's budget (circulation revenue), and which is totally free of journalistic ethics and standards. The Internet, and particularly "social media," is utterly devoid of any standards or control and is the medium for crackpots, fanatics, criminals, and crazies of every variety. The electorate is bombarded with both information and disinformation, and only the educated segment of U.S. readers is capable of sorting it out. The recent election certainly raises a serious question about the size of America's literate, perceptive public.

So let's aim our hopes (and more revenue), at U.S. schools of Journalism and U.S. newsrooms. They have to function first, before government watchdogs swing into action (if there are any of them left after Donald "drains the swamp").

The Fourth Estate has saved America in the past. I hope they can rise to the occasion and do it again.

1/11/17

A Belligerent Buffoon

Most buffoons are funny, at least part of the time. This one isn't.

He is unhinged, impulsive, self-focused, and belligerent, all at once. Add to that collection of adjectives uninformed, if not ignorant. What he doesn't know in history and economics (yes, economics), would make up an education.

All of the Nobelists in Economics and History are simply shaking their heads in disbelief. Of course, they are all located on the two coasts, so have no idea of the level of intellect in Red America.

Aside from fearing for the future of the U.S. after another year or two of this belligerent blowhard, I guess we should empathize with the small core of intellects who sought refuge on university campuses in NASCAR America.

Fortunately, American journalists are already on the march against the shocking new wave of tinhorn tyranny … and constitutional lawyers are scratching their heads over the best route to injunctions now, and possibly impeachment down the road. If the Donald does continue an assault on almost all political institutions and come to be regarded as truly a mental case—which many of us realized long before November 8—the provisions of the 25th Amendment may come into play for the first time.

However, the present language of that Amendment requires a vote of 2/3 of both Houses to replace the President—and then the office would fall to the Vice President, meaning Donald's handsome, Neolithic, boot licking minion, Michael Pence.

So we would be only half way home to a stable, functioning USA. And the chances of the Republican House and Senate voting that Donald is "unable to discharge the powers and duties of his office" are probably nil, even if Donald gets wild-eyed and foams at the mouth.

So in the meanwhile all we can do is to invoke a new lexicon of adjectives for an agitated, abusive buffoon and hope that five or ten Republican Senators call an end to the bedlam and disarray we have already seen in just two weeks.

2/5/17

Fasten Your Seatbelts:
Corruption Just Ahead

OUR TWEETER-IN-CHIEF PROMISED TO "drain the swamp" in Washington, D.C. and to clean out the thicket of regulations on Wall Street. His stated goal is to rid us of all the bureaucratic regulations that are hampering America's precious free enterprise system. He tells us that the red tape created by big government do-gooders has made life tough for his entrepreneurial friends and cost American jobs. As a successful big-time businessman—(six bankruptcies)—he knows what American industry wants and needs .

He started his attack on the Environmental Protection Agency by nominating an avowed enemy of that body to be its Chairman. Scott Pruitt's history has been to sue the EPA and threaten to dismantle it. So much for the Clean Air Act, and solutions for acid rain and greenhouse gasses.

Then he wants Congress to repeal Dodd-Frank

and the banking regulations adopted since the 2008 recession as a safeguard against another financial crash. Lots of luck on that one.

Now he intends to scuttle the so-called "fiduciary rule," which requires financial advisers to put their clients' interests ahead of their own and to avoid conflicts of interest which have reportedly cost retirement funds an estimated 17 billion dollars annually.

He is appointing as Chairman of the Federal Communications Commission an individual who opposes the "net neutrality" rule for Internet service providers, an Obama policy favored by Google, Netflix, and other large websites, but opposed by Trump supporters like AT&T and Comcast. There goes fairness in Internet production.

In short, Donald wants to clear the path for enterprising businessmen like him, so they can increase profits and thereby create more jobs for his fans in Red America and The Rust Belt. Maybe he will get around to the Sherman Act and the Clayton Act, which laws were born to break up and prevent cartels and oligarchies in the early Twentieth century. Or he can persuade the Antitrust Division of the Department of Justice to sit on their hands like they did for eight years under George W. Bush.

Shades of 1929 and 2008. It's probably not a coincidence that our two major depressions followed eight years of Republican free market philosophy.

Republicans instinctively shrink from regulation and believe that what's good for an American businessman is good for America.

But bitter experience has proven that what's good for business is good for America only if a set of rules is imposed, rules conceived after generations of experience with the multiple facets of human nature. There will always be Charles Ponzi's and Bernie Madoff's waiting in the wings for lack of oversight and feeble regulation.

As long as we still need stop signs and homicide laws and burglary laws in our neighborhoods, we will need some sophisticated oversight in our financial and political world, because human beings come in all forms, all the way from teddy bears to coyotes. And the coyotes are always out there waiting, just out of sight.

So if Donald eliminates too much "red tape" and governmental "strangulation," in the name of free enterprise, I strongly suggest that you go into caveat emptor mode, marshal and monitor your assets, and develop a Plan B if the U.S. degrades into a political and economic free-for-all .

2/12/17

A Part of Your Memory
that Won't Fail

WHILE SKIING MERRILY DOWN a slope at Sierra Ski
Ranch, a little ahead of a somewhat-more-cau-
tious Maralys behind me, I caught an edge with my
right ski and was unceremoniously pitched to the
ground on my right side. When M. approached she
routinely asked if I was all right.

This time I couldn't say I was OK, because my
right shoulder wasn't. It wasn't all right because I had
suffered what a lot of football players get, an acromio-
clavicular separation, usually called a shoulder separation. The outer clavicle head was separated from the
acromion, the basic shoulder joint or pad.

A painful night in South Lake Tahoe and trip
home was an unprecedented end to one of our many
ski weekends at Heavenly and Kirkwood, but I assumed
it would be nothing but a memory after a week or two.

Not to be. A fly fishing excursion to a friend's

ranch on the Madison River in Montana fired up the shoulder again—it didn't like that ten o'clock-to-two o'clock arc that is prescribed by genuine fly fishermen. Hemorrhage preceded a surgery known as acromioplasty, and we figured that was the end of the shoulder problem.

Again, not to be. Who would have expected an a-c separation and an acromioplasty to lead, 28 years later, to regular nocturnal reminders of an ancient almost-routine injury? What we didn't know in our youth—and even in those very active middle years—is that your body has a memory of certain insults, a memory better than yours if you live long enough.

The inevitable and progressive osteoarthritis creates all sorts of new aches and pains as you progress in the 80s and 90s, but it gets worse in some areas of long-since-forgotten trauma, sometimes going back to adolescence.

For example, a shin scar I got from a surfboard at Waikiki in 1941 (just before we had to take our boards through barbed wire after 12/7/41—but that's another story...) seems to grow in size 75 years later. And a length of surgical wire left in my left flank after a nephrolithotomy in 1972 still worries radiologists and occasionally speaks to nerves in the flank area.

But the one trauma that speaks loudest about the body's memory was that a-c separation 28 years ago, which didn't get resolved by surgery and now produces symptoms in the shoulder and right hand that actually affect sleep.

I doubt that many pro football players will live deep into their 80s and 90s, but if they do, I can guarantee that they will have a medicine cabinet full of anti-inflammatory drugs and pain killers. The new risk will be opioid addiction or insomnia, or both. Instead of "better living through chemistry," it will be survival through pharmacology.

That damned right shoulder is one of several dozen reasons why I'm glad I have a partner at age 89, especially one with massage skills. And also why I own stock in 123 pharmacology and biotechnology companies.

3/18/17

INVESTMENT ADVICE TO ERICA

E RICA,
   I'm not a devotee of mutual funds and deal almost exclusively in individual stocks. My investment decisions are based on copious reading—in nonfiction only—especially in areas of special interest, like medicine, pharmacology, energy, and environment.

We do own a few mutual funds in those fields, Fidelity MSCI Health Care (FHLC), Fidelity Select Medical Equipment (FSMEX), Fidelity Select Health Care (FSPHX), and Fidelity Select Biotechnology, (FBIOX). They are reliable, but not exciting.

Christy had a gang of Berkeley pals at Chris' ranch last week and one of them, a Brit, saw me going over Annual Reports and signing proxies, so he asked me my investment "strategy." I told him it is anything but technical or strategic. I simply read a lot in a lot of areas, watch CNBC in the A.M., and basically focus on the horizon, not the present.

Certain world trends are obvious and unavoidable. Huge populations are aging and will get sick. Everyone is health-conscious and treatment-"entitled." Three or four areas of the globe are overpopulated, under-educated, and headed for disaster (famine, epidemics, water-deprivation, and civil unrest—revolution or migration). Start with all the of sub-Saharan Africa, the Middle East, and Southeast Asia.

The grim geopolitical horizon clearly points to pharmacology (the U.S. is thoroughly drug-oriented, legal and illegal), Agchem (seed and fertilizer advances), Hydrology (very few stocks there), medical equipment and supplies (lots of stocks there), and defense (we have seven strong defense stocks).

Those categories make up a large percentage of our portfolio, but we own stock in 15 utilities (fairly safe, with good yield), 5 solid food companies, several Amazon-proof retailers (Costco, Lowe's, Home Depot), and a few A-rated industrials, like GE, Emerson Electric, Honeywell, Kimberly-Clark, and Proctor and Gamble.

I can't recommend railroad stocks, but we do own 6 (Norfolk-Southern is a very good one), and our bumbling President should be good for them.

This is a longer answer than I gave Christy's friend, but it gives me a chance to explain my investment "strategy," such as it is.

I don't give advice on investing in stocks because I

violate all traditional investment rules (except diversity), and realize that the market faces ever-greater geopolitical instability, is a form of semi-professional gambling, and is definitely not for everyone.

Many should stick to real estate, which is slow but steady (too slow for me). Many others should stick to mutual funds (Fidelity or Vanguard), get an ETF (exchange-traded fund), or get the best CD available.

I'm glad you asked, though. It gave me a chance to expand on last week's answer, and it tells me that you and Christian have big wads of money to invest.

Bob —5/1/17

ANYONE READY FOR REFORM?
CALIFORNIA HAS A PRIME CANDIDATE

I'M JUST REVIEWING a graphic report on the California prison system, and I find the statistics way past alarming to mind-boggling. I wish that every California voter knew them before they went to the polls, or even a town hall meeting. I wonder if the California Legislators try to deal with these numbers, but I suspect they regard the problem as nearly hopeless, a political bombshell to be dealt with only when social activist organizations get a Federal Court Order on constitutional grounds, as they did several years ago.

As I recall, the Federal Order came because the severe overcrowding of California prisons—at 179.5 percent of design capacity in 2001—violated the Eighth Amendment of the U.S. Constitution, which prohibits "cruel and unusual punishment."

The State did respond to the Federal mandate by getting some new laws—including by Initiative—that redefined felonies and shortened sentences in various ways. The new laws resulted this year in a reduction in overcrowding to 131.9 percent of design capacity. This still means four prisoners confined in space designed for three. We'll see how long before compliance with the Federal Order is again policed and enforced further.

That 131.9 percent of design capacity equals 118,382 California felons housed in 34 State Prisons located all the way from the Oregon border (Pelican Bay), to San Diego. Of that 118,383 only 5222 are women. And those numbers don't include 4,253 California felons imprisoned at California expense in for-profit prisons in Arizona and Mississippi.

State prisons house only convicted felons, not the tens of thousands currently imprisoned by Cities and Counties for misdemeanor convictions.

And here come three mind-blowing statistics that caught me flat-footed. The reported annual cost to incarcerate a California felon in one of those huge facilities is now $70,812, which is three times what I thought it was. That includes 19 items of cost, with the largest single item, "security," being $32,019 per prisoner. "Security" does not include food or medical or supplies or building operating expense, so I assume it primarily covers the salaries of the guards and other security staff.

Which leads us to the second shocker. California and New Jersey are the only states where prison guards are paid "$70,000 and up" per year. Most of the other states pay guards $34,000 to $49,999 per year, and some even less, meaning that the average California prison guard makes double the salary of a guard in most other states—and California has the largest prison population in the U.S., so the numbers are huge.

So while the Legislature and the electorate were urged to redefine felonies and lighten sentencing, they obviously didn't tinker with the pay scales of the richest prison guards in the world. And those salaries make up about half of the $11 billion California spends annually on the prison system.

If you do some rough math, it seems that California prison guards take up something like 4 percent of California's total $124 billion budget. If that isn't a sign of dystopia, I don't know what is. It's almost medieval in essence.

The final shocker is as depressing as it is shocking. California has a 61 percent recidivism rate among its inmates. Thus, we not only have a huge prison population, the largest in the world, but we also have a failing criminal justice correction system. Almost 2 out of 3 of those 122, 636 inmates now costing us $70, 812 per year will be back in the system again—to join all the thousands of new felons sentenced annually.

Anyone see any reason for reform of a system like this? And, more pointedly, does anyone see any HOPE for reform of such a huge and broken segment of our society?

5/11/17

Why California May Soon
Stand Alone

T HE TELEVISION AND PRESS political coverage
obviously focuses on Washington, D.C., where
the Tweeter-in-Chief and the GOP conservatives
are running the show, in complete control of all three
branches of government (now including the Supreme
Court). The Democrats are reduced to protesting and
finger-pointing, but won't win a vote on anything
important for years.

Obama's eight-year governmental structure is
slowly but surely being dismantled by a party that
basically dislikes and distrusts government per se.
Ronald Reagan is alive and well, not only with the Tea
Party and Freedom Caucus nut cases, but with Trump's
Redneck Revolution as well. ("Government can't solve
the problem: government IS the problem").

But the war against government is being waged
and won much more quietly and effectively at the state

level, where Republicans occupy 33 of the 50 Governor's Mansions and control 60 of the 99 Legislative chambers. That's 66 percent control of the executive and legislative branches, far more dominance than in Washington, D.C. And the real shocker comes when you learn that half of the American State governments are Republican trifectas, meaning that the GOP controls both the Governor's mansion and BOTH houses of the legislature.

So you can imagine what is happening to so-called "liberal" or "progressive" (or Democratic) programs in the trifecta states. They're dead on arrival and slowly being erased from the books. And with 2/3 of the legislatures and 2/3 of the Governor's mansions being Republican, you can imagine where the Koch brothers and the conservative PAC's are spending their money, now that they have succeeded in seating Donald Trump, the Tea Party, and the Freedom Caucus in Washington, D.C.

A perfect example is a PAC called ALEC, known to every state legislator for years now. It stands for American Legislative Exchange Council, and is funded by the Koch brothers, Walmart, AT&T, and Exxon Mobil. ALEC drafts and sponsors "model" legislation, which it then gets promoted by its well-supported key legislators.

The ALEC legislation very cleverly employs a process called "preemption," which results in state laws overruling any conflicting county or city legislation. The ALEC model legislation has been adopted verbatim in dozens of states and used to nullify progressive ordinances in states like Wisconsin, Ohio, Texas, and North Carolina. In fact, the Governor of Texas has proposed a shotgun Texas law designed to preempt ALL local regulations in one fell swoop, so that all "progressive" or "liberal" regulations or ordinances would be automatically annulled from Austin, virtually eliminating any local Texas legislation not acceptable to the Republican Governor and legislature.

The power brokers long ago concluded that they could achieve their political and economic goals much more efficiently and economically by controlling State capitols than by financing Federal elections. So when Donald Trump created the Redneck Revolution last Fall, some of the ALEC leaders crowed out loud about their opportunity to focus their dollars and their strategy on Statehouses, with Washington, D.C. in safe libertarian hands.

But the Statehouse Mafia apparently haven't found a soft spot in Sacramento, where the trifecta is securely on the Democratic side of the fence. They would dearly love to get control of the sixth largest economy in THE WORLD, so you know they won't fade away for long. California is too big a prize for the Libertarians, Tea Partiers, Free Traders, Freedom Caucus, and Neocons to give up on.

We've lost Washington, D.C. Let's at least hang on to Sacramento.

6/2/17

THE U.S. POLITICAL LANDSCAPE: Where to Place Your Bets

THE DEMOCRATS AND THEIR blood brothers can have all the speeches, marches, and Town Halls they want, then spend a billion or two dollars on the 2018 elections in the campaign against a Trump plutocracy. But the only hope of really changing the direction of the U.S. government lies elsewhere. Even in the unlikely event that the Democrats retake the House or Senate, we will still have either a blowhard lightweight or a mossback Bible-slapper in the White House.

It's the third arm of government that will probably dominate our social, political, and economic course for the next five or ten years, because any big issues in those areas will probably run into a conflict between a dysfunctional Congress and an incompetent or Neolithic White House. And you know where big conflicts involving big issues are destined to end up in an increasingly polemic and litigious society: of course, the U.S. Supreme Court.

The age, health, and political posture of the 9 members of SCOTUS are the real key to the political future of the country. The Republican Senators knew this when they prevented Obama, by foul means, from appointing a replacement for Antonin Scalia in 2016. They knew a Republican president would appoint a true blue Conservative. I'm sure they were delighted when The Donald appointed a truly predictable ultra-conservative Gorsuch. And he has already demonstrated his stripes.

The recent four special elections, all won by Republicans, tell us that the East and West Coast intelligentsia still don't comprehend the Redneck Revolution of 2016. It may get harder now to raise money for Democratic candidates, because the party is now baffled and dispirited. Trump is nothing if he's not a talented rabble rouser. And what a lot of liberal intellectuals are now beginning to realize is that the U.S. has hordes of disenchanted rabble to rouse. (Something I learned in the U.S. Army).

If you want to focus on the most critical political factors in the next few years, focus on the age and health of 3 members of SCOTUS, Kennedy, Ginsburg, and Breyer. The three of them are very elderly—Ginsburg, 84, Kennedy, 80, and Breyer, almost 79—and at some risk of death or stroke. The same three would, I suspect, accept retirement if a reasonable replacement was available. In fact, there is speculation about Justice Kennedy retiring soon, and he is the most reliable swing vote.

The four conservative justices, all appointed by Republican presidents, are all relatively young, except Thomas, who is 69. I can't see Thomas leaving except on a stretcher, and the two Obama ladies are young (ish), 63 and 57, and healthy.

So if you are placing bets on the future direction of the U.S., either before or after the 2018 elections, study the medical records and lifestyles of Ginsburg, Kennedy, and Breyer, and maybe put a hex on Fellow Traveler Thomas. A loss of any of the three oldest members of SCOTUS will seal our fate (and hasten our move to Costa Rica).

6/30/17

THE MEDIA AND MARKETING MONSTERS: Not Just Social Disruption and Mercantile Domination

IF YOU ARE WORRIED about the effect that the huge media giants, Amazon, Google, and Facebook, are having on the fabric of American society, I think you are more than justified. Social media are eroding the family unit through perpetual and irresistible distraction, replacing familial discourse and counseling with electronic intercourse and social fetish.

The average parent today only thinks he controls and molds his offspring. His power may be reduced to financial and material deprivation, a series of pleas and threats, risking alienation or subterfuge (or departure). In most families, the age-old support of church, YMCA, Boy Scouts, Girl Scouts, and family net-working are history.

Which means that the average teen now spends far more time on Facebook, Instagram, and other social media sites than with parents or siblings, and gets most of his or her mores and credo from electronic friends and strangers.

The parental reporting is rife with tales of attempts to limit or muffle the social media invasion of the family dinner table, or living room, or family car, but most are doomed to failure. Teenage social media addiction is here and not amenable to rehab. The iPhone is almost every teenager's best friend.

The reach of Amazon is a different type of threat. Not only did Bezos and Co. wipe out 90 percent of the book stores in the U.S.—Borders and almost all but Barnes & Noble—but now Amazon is imperiling large and small general stores, including big box grocery marketers, and is a threat to malls across the U.S. and your local hardware store. E-commerce, particularly Amazon, is changing the face of American retailing. It may present a short term benefit in pricing and delivery convenience. But beware the long term effect of Bezos' stranglehold on commerce.

Not having teenage children or retail price concerns, we don't worry about the social or marketing impact of America's corporate giants as much as sociologists, psychologists, and economists should. But there's another effect of their size and power that is extremely worrisome for me, and that's their effect on our last line of defense in a collapsing, chaotic society—our free press.

What only journalists and political scientists may have noticed is that the three corporate giants have swallowed up a huge chunk of America's advertising budget, and a "free press" is not free. It depends on the advertising revenue that is being gobbled up by Facebook and Google and the other social media sites that are financed (and enriched) by the ads they plant in their streaming.

In a political structure now shot through with deception, corruption, and duplicity, not to mention dysfunction, the role of investigative journalism has never been so important (except perhaps during Harding and Nixon). But the Bernsteins and Woodwards don't come free, nor do the editors and printing presses behind them.

I knew years ago that journalism budgets were down because the Internet cut sharply into newspaper circulation (and thereby income). Small to medium newspapers failed, or were gobbled up. Even the biggies, like the *New York Times* and *Los Angeles Times*, had newsroom cuts before the social media drain began.

But I was shocked this week to read that newspaper advertising revenue plummeted from $50 billion in 2006 to $18 billion in 2016, ten years later. That's a 64 percent drop in an age when we need MORE journalism, not less. The number of jobs in journalism dropped from 411,000 in 2001 to 174,000 in 2016, a 58 percent drop.

Who is going to go into investigative journalism with Google and Facebook eating up so much of the advertising revenue? And if we don't train and motivate more Woodwards and Bernsteins, who is going to save this country from the demagoguery and corruption and deception that are staring us in the face in August, 2017?

I'll tell you one thing: it won't be politicians and it won't be attorneys and it won't be the military. It will be the group that Hitler and all other tyrants target first. That would be investigative journalism, my friends.

RVW

THE TIME BOMB NO WALL CAN BLOCK

SOMEONE ONCE WROTE A book entitled *While America Slept,* lamenting America's isolationism while the Nazi menace bloomed in Europe. We know now how that period of self-focus worked out. Millions died, including 416,800 Americans, all over the globe.

A blowhard rabble-rouser has now mobilized tens of millions in Red America in a new "America First" campaign, combining nostalgia, xenophobia, and disaffection under the slogan "Make America Great Again." He touts a wall, immigration restrictions, and trade tariffs as methods to make America safe and prosperous again. He warns that Mexican immigrants, Chinese trade practices, and Muslim terrorists are a scourge that threatens our beloved America.

Most Americans now know that Donald Trump is a fraud and his promise to make America safe again is a cruel hoax. What demographers know, and Red America will learn too late, is that there is a ticking time bomb growing in sub-Saharan Africa, the Middle East, and Southeast Asia that will darken America's future far more than Adolph Hitler and Hideki Tojo did 75 years ago.

The ticking time bomb is a population explosion occurring in the poorest and most volatile areas of this shrinking planet—in Nigeria, the Congo, Ethiopia, Yemen, Burundi, Liberia, Niger, Bangladesh, Indonesia, and other countries not far from the equator. The Director of the CIA got no publicity when he warned that the population of these equatorial countries is now expected to triple by 2050, with Ethiopia, Nigeria, and Yemen doubling. The silent demographers predict that world population will increase from 7 ½ billion to 10 billion by 2050—an increase greater than the current populations of China and India combined.

The other fact that scares the demographers is that the bulk of the increase will consist of young people in poorly governed countries, a deadly combination. Nothing makes for a riskier powder keg than hundreds of millions of young people without enough food and water in a country with a weak or corrupt government. Europe got a taste of the problem in 2016 and this year, when hundreds of thousands got across the Mediterranean and literally invaded Greece, Italy, Hungary, Germany, France, and Scandinavia.

Except for Central and South America, the U.S. is protected by a saltwater moat, the Atlantic and Pacific oceans, so it will be a lot harder to cross than the Mediterranean was last year. But the world is shrinking and who knows how big the boats would have to be to cross from West Africa to Brazil, a crossing of 1600 miles (from Senegal to NE Brazil). And if hundreds of thousands did somehow make that crossing, Trump's ten billion dollar wall would be no obstacle to a militant horde who regard America as the land of milk and honey.

Probably the greater risk from the militant and malnourished millions still to arrive on our planet is the risk of invasion into one or more of our NATO or SEATO allies in Europe or Southeast Asia. How far would the U.S. go to protect an ally from an invading horde, especially if we still have an "America First" regime in Washington? Time will tell, but for the time being Trump & Co. are focusing on the immediate risk, which is violence in the U.S. from Islamic or disaffected terrorists or missiles from a rogue or renegade U.S. antagonist across those oceans.

Thanks to Melinda Gates, a Catholic, who now recognizes and announces that family planning (including birth control), is the only solution to the overpopulation and under endowment threat in the Third World. Family planning is a much cheaper solution to over population than war. In fact, it and technology—agricultural and hydrologic—are the only solutions to the ticking time bomb overseas.

Too bad that George W. Bush and Donald Trump and the Republican Congress didn't recognize that fact when they adopted, and then re-adopted, the so-called Mexico City Rule, which cuts off all U.S. support for international family planning. That policy alone seriously threatens the future of our 13 great grandchildren and billions of humans.

9/29/17

A Lifetime: First and Last it's Medical

A HUMAN IS BORN as a medical event. If all goes well, the medical issues are soon forgotten. Psychological and social issues predominate.

The last chapter is also a medical event. Hopefully a brief one. But more often an extended one, often a painful or disabling one. Medical issues and developments dominate the fade-out. Everything else is trivial.

That is, assuming you have adequate resources to maintain a comfortable board and room, and to afford the best medical care available at that time and place.

If not, the end becomes a medical process exacerbated by economics. A nasty combination to end the adventure.

DECEMBER, 2017

WITH RARE EXCEPTIONS, ANYONE reading this report lives in Blue America. If you haven't seen the political map of the U.S., Blue America is the states on the West Coast and those from Maine down to Virginia on the East Coast. The rest of the country voted in Donald Trump and a Republican Congress.

The lines of demarcation between Red America and Blue America are not just political. They tend to be cultural and religious as well. People in Kansas and Mississippi don't read the NY Times or the LA Times or The Washington Post or The Week, or anything else published by the "liberal media" on the coasts. So we shouldn't be shocked when we read interviews revealing that many of those in Red America still think that Trump is doing a "good job" and is just being picked on by the "liberal media"....

A year ago we assumed that 2017 was going to be a chaotic, if not tumultuous, year. It wasn't either of those, but it was fascinating to all and alarming to some. The question in our minds is whether Trump is merely wreaking his revenge on Barack Obama for ridiculing him publicly—by acting to undo every Obama program—or whether he really does have Fascist tendencies that remind a lot of elder Americans of the coming of The Third Reich in the 1930s.

We have German friends who remember Hitler's hatred of the press, the courts, and the intellectual elite, and how he ultimately shut them down. Sound familiar? I'm sure that Trump is scariest to historians and people over 80 who remember the past. He is certainly scary to my partner and her closest friends.

At the age of 90 my attention falls primarily into 3 categories: medical, financial, and travel. It's a rare bird in our age group that doesn't have two or three nagging medical problems, and a string of doctors' appointments. M's medical year included a hysterectomy and cystectomy in March, followed by some mysterious "nerve pain" that keeps her on analgesics. If that fades and Trump gets impeached, she'll be fine.

The cruise last January was in honor of the 65th birthday of both Chris and Betty Jo. Then Chris retired from office practice this Fall, partly induced by a neuropathy in his right arm (possibly going back to a neck injury at Caneel Bay Plantation in 1977). Can you imagine being old enough to see your children retiring?

As you can see from the photos, 2017 treated

us very well indeed. Trips to the Caribbean, Kauai, Virginia, and Scotland made it a very rich year, and the "Trump" stock market made it a very fruitful year. I don't know how long the bull market can last—I don't think the actual U.S. economy supports it—but I'll ride it as long as it does. And share some of it with the next two generations.

Our trip to Scotland turned out to be an amazing success. Our granddaughter, Lauren, and her husband, Dan, made the trip a rare one, even for travel vets like us. I was just the Tour Producer and CFO. Lauren was the Floor Manager, Reservations Manager, Photographer, Transportation Manager, and Historian (a beautiful Apple photo book with text). Dan was the Property Manager, Head Waiter, and Caregiver.

Oh yes, and Maralys was the Tour Celebrity Author and Social Butterfly. All in all, a great team and a bonnie introduction to Loch Ness, Pitlochry, the whiskey distilleries, Edinburgh, York, and London. For details, see M's blog about the trip.

The trip to Norfolk was highlighted by the commissioning of Erica's husband, Christian Carpenter, as a 2nd Lieutenant in the U.S. Marine Corp. Christian is a college graduate, has been to Afghanistan, and completed the Marine equivalent of Navy Seal, so he's an all-around asset to the Marine Corps. As always, Ken and Melanie threw a great party for the occasion.

One of my birthday cards announced that "There

are many nice things to be said about growing older." Inside it says "Most of them are lies." I think the author of the card has been there, but also realizes that old age beats the alternative by a mile. And since we're here, we may as well make the most of it and focus on the good parts. And as you can see from the photos, there are a lot of good parts.

For your sake and ours, we hope that the two nut cases in the news —Donald and Kim Jung Un—don't run off the rails and contaminate part of planet Earth. Maybe that dysfunctional Congress will get organized and install some security measures around the nuclear button. No one human should have the power to irradiate millions, least of all The Donald.

I'm looking out at a blue sky, our green woodland, and some beautiful colored leaves. I just had a Royal Riviera pear. And we have a Pacific Symphony concert in four hours, with prime seats. So things can't be all bad, can they?

Rob McWills

A Flimsy Argument Built on a False Premise

Has anyone in this dyspeptic, dysphoric, dysfunctional country other than legal scholars ever read the oft-quoted Second Amendment, either literally or figuratively? Apparently not, because ninety percent of the endless argument about gun control is firmly based on the false premise that the 27 words of the Second Amendment give every U.S. citizen an unfettered right to own and use firearms of every type and in any manner he or she desires.

They don't. Not even close.

First, take a look at the exact language of this shibboleth and then interpret those words in the context of the environment and the language in which it was written.

Like most language in the U.S. Constitution, the Second Amendment is terse. "A well regulated Militia being necessary to the security of a free State, the right of the people to keep and bear Arms, shall not be infringed ...."

Note the word "Militia," with a capital M. Then look up the English word "militia" in your dictionary. It means either a group of soldiers, an "organized militia," or a group of citizens called up to secure the government in a time of emergency, an "unorganized militia," consisting of males between the age of 18 and 45. Note that " militia" has the same root as military.

Then note that this "right" was drafted by American patriots at a time when the Colonies had been at war with Great Britain and had no army or navy or marine corps or coast guard, or even national guard. This was the period between 1787, when the Constitution itself was adopted, and 1789, when the Second Amendment was adopted as part of the Bill of Rights (the first ten amendments).

So the framers of the Bill of Rights, recalling the Revolutionary War, clearly felt that armed male citizens would constitute an unorganized national guard in 1789, in case another foreign power attacked (Spain, Mexico, or whoever).

Also please note the second most important word in the Second Amendment: "Arms." As any good Constitutional Law professor would testify, a law or statute should be interpreted in the context of the time and the state of the language in which it was drafted. What did "Arms" mean in 1789? It meant a long-barreled musket that required priming for each ball shot, or possibly a one-shot dueling pistol. I leave it to an arms historian to describe the state of "arms" in 1789, but I can safely declare that "Arms" did not include an automatic or semiautomatic rifle, a revolver, or even a double-barreled shotgun. Obviously, the number of people a crazed militiaman could kill in 1789 was uno.

So a good constitutional lawyer could probably argue successfully that his physically fit male between 18 and 45 years of age cannot have his right to own a musket or a dueling pistol infringed, even though the U.S. already has several forms of "organized militia" in millions of uniforms ready to meet any emergency, and even though a lot of the "unorganized militia" in the U.S. today would clearly dodge being called up as an emergency militia in 2018 (Canada is still an option.)

But I don't know how any U.S. citizen could successfully challenge any federal, state, or even local law banning his or her ownership of any weapon that could be considered a danger to the public safety and common good—any automatic or semi-automatic or revolving or repeater or bullet clip weapon. Leave it to the muskets, sabers, and swords that any physically fit male could own, store, and cherish in 1789. And leave it to the now-enormous "organized militia" to maintain 'the security of a free State"

2/23/18

FORBIDDEN AMBROSIA

I SUSPECT THAT THERE is a lode of brilliant wit, gratifying insights, and cozy empathy out there somewhere for two kindred spirits who hunger for some sensory excitement and find each other appetizing.

If the potential lovers are not already spoken for, the only requirement would be a friendly twist of fate in their meeting on a planet swarming with seven billion humans. The mathematical odds against that are almost infinitesimal, but sometimes fate or karma or dumb luck may put two soul mates in one place at the same time.

If the star-struck pair already have spouses, the challenge reaches a new magnitude. The question becomes whether they can savor that trove of pleasure without inflicting collateral damage on their wards and dependents. Neither middle class society nor marital partners are forgiving when it comes to extramarital emotional and physical coupling. All prior fidelity and nobility are quickly forgotten if the forbidden coupling is discovered and attacked.

So to survive, the union must remain clandestine. And if it becomes all-consuming, the chances of that happening are slim to none.

So Shangri-La usually comes at a very high cost.

6/28/17

A Celestial Coalescence of Talent and Discipline

There's one surefire way for me to escape the tawdry parade of political and social disarray I watch daily on the TV screen and in the public arena. That's a concert of classical music by an illustrious orchestra and soloist.

Last night the transport was provided by Andre Watt and the Pacific Symphony playing Beethoven's Emperor concerto (#5) in Segerstrom Symphony Hall. That concerto is particularly rhapsodic and pulsating and, as they learned in Carnegie Hall last week, the Pacific Symphony is now a world-class orchestra with a world-class conductor (a protégé of Leonard Bernstein).

And Andre Watt is a phenomenon himself, playing those thousands of notes flawlessly at age 77 (when my hands are so arthritic I can hardly write these notes with a pen).

The fact that Ludwig Von Beethoven could

write that music in 1811—207 years ago—and those hundred and more residents of Orange County and environs could play the concerto in perfect precision for 45 minutes—proves to me that there is still hope for the human race, despite the nauseating displays in Washington, D.C. and red America, and despite the squalor and misery rife in the Third World (which is laid in front of us nightly on that big TV screen).

I get the same reaction every time I hear a symphony or concerto written in the eighteenth or nineteenth century by Beethoven or Brahms or Tchaikovsky or Rachmaninoff, but much less so with Gershwin or Copeland or most modern composers. I suspect that as life became more discordant and frenetic in the last century so did the serious music.

Where except in a concert hall can you see a hundred dedicated artists performing with perfect precision and several hundred citizens sitting quietly and listening? The closest example today would probably be a lecture in a university classroom, but I can't think of any others in an increasingly strident, agitated, and coarse population here and abroad.

Aside from three or four trips a year to more exotic or quaint retreats, and a steady diet of British television drama, the concert hall remains one place where I can temporarily forget the decadence and decay we witness on the news every night and read in our numerous newspapers and magazines.

But I do often wonder how long classical music will survive, even though it has survived for centuries already. Our ten grandkids and thirteen great grandkids know very little about it and will probably have a lot more pressing and a lot more turbulent issues facing them in this century.

5/4/18

An America We Don't Often See

TODAY I SPENT TWO hours in an environment that
few of my social class have ever seen up close and
personal. It was an experience I'm still trying to evaluate.

There are jokes about the California Department
of Motor Vehicles being a jungle or a zoo. But few
people I know have ever been there, at least in the last
five or 10 years. I was in the Santa Ana DMV office two
or three times many years ago, to pass a driving test or
renew my driver's license. But it was nothing like it is
now, just as California, and even the U.S., are not much
like they were 20 years ago.

A DMV visit then took something like an hour
or two, with no line outside and with numbers called
for a seated waiting area inside. I needed my driver's
license renewed after five years and gave up trying to
make an appointment by phone. That failed effort
should have given me a clue that times have changed.
So I decided to give the project a good piece of this

afternoon, although I'd heard about long lines.

Driving around the building at First and Grand gave me an idea of what I was facing. There was a line maybe 150 feet long outside a door marked "No Appointment." Then, on the other side, there was a line of a hundred or more strung along outside a door that was marked "Appointment Only." I knew that neither line was for me.

So I parked and sidled through the "Appointment" door and found dozens already inside and seated, waiting to be called after checking in. Looking as old and as lame as I could, with my cane as a mouthpiece, I told one of the women behind the check-in desk how impossible my phone effort had been and that I was not able to stand in line. She told me to sit down and gave me a blue sheet that simply said "wants to make an appointment." She said it could be quite awhile before they could get to me. All I was going to get today was an appointment for another trip later.

Long story short. By a combination of luck, observation, and finesse, I ended up getting a number in a group who all had appointments already and were also disabled.

After an hour of dismayed and disturbing observation of the mass of humanity around me, and the patience of two DMV employees I later wrote up with a commendation card, I got the application filled out in the computer room, paid the $35 renewal fee, passed the eye test (even without glasses), and passed the six-page written exam. After two hours of very mixed emotions, I walked out with my temporary license—even though my thumb would not give a print on three different fingerprint sensors. (That baffled three different, very patient employees.)

Had I left that building with no license after the first hour and a half, I would have painted you a very grim picture of the America your grandchildren will be facing. In fact, it would have matched the picture of America that many of the 62 million who elected Trump would have painted.

I can easily appreciate why those "red" Americans would love to "Make America Great Again," because that mob today didn't look anything like the Vermonters and Bostonians I grew up with 75 and 80 years ago.

But neither Trump nor his flunkies is going to Make America White Again. And after working with three or four of those "alien" Americans in that jungle today, I moderated my visceral reaction almost completely. I realized that my discomfort was a product of racial disparity, extreme numbers, and unfamiliarity with wholesale destitution. I just didn't see my country, my culture, my contemporaries looking like that.

But a lot of it does. And believe it or not, the California vehicle registration system does work overall, despite the zoo appearance (and the fact I had to finesse the system). I guess America will go on for awhile.

But it just won't look much like it used to. Those of my generation will simply have to adjust to it. It may not be a pretty picture. It will clearly take an attitude adjustment. But we either adjust or flee.

And, frankly, I see no haven that will overall pass ours as a home base. We'll just have to ride out the melting pot disruption and the Trump dismantlement campaign. There is no Shangri-La overseas or Xanadu here. But with enough resources and ingenuity we can still wall off most of the social turmoil and political decay that we watch on the tube every night.

5/8/18

TRAVEL SHINES AGAIN

W E HAVE JUST RETURNED from a whirlwind trip to Europe that renewed my respect for travel and for a high level of organization. The scheduled portion of the junket involved Scotland, Wales, Dublin, and Normandy, starting in Glasgow and ending on the Omaha Beach portion of Normandy (literally with David and Julie Eisenhower).

As you know, we travel a great deal, averaging at least 3 sorties a year. I have traveled all my life, because of a military father and a snowbird mother ("snowbird" meaning she headed south at the first snowfall). So I spent my youth in Massachusetts, Vermont, Florida, Panama, California, Hawaii, and Montana. Then, as an adult with family, there were almost countless trips to Europe, the Caribbean, and Hawaii.

The first forty years were privately organized, rarely involving even a travel agent. But since the QE 2 voyage in 1988, there have been nine or 10 ocean cruises and two European river cruises, ranging from St. Petersburg to Buenos Aires to Sydney, and only recently has an AAA travel agent been involved.

This heavily organized and well managed expedition was only our second arranged through the UCLA Alumni Association, which has offered countless exotic (and educational) excursions over the years. Our first was a good look at Costa Rica many years ago. This one was called the "Celtic Lands" tour and covered the Scottish Highlands, the Hebrides, Wales, Dublin, and the 74th anniversary of D-Day on and along Omaha Beach in Normandy. The travel organizer was a Chicago firm we didn't know—Gohagan Co.—and the accommodation was a small 5-star French ship called Le Boreal.

The featured lecturers were David Eisenhower (Dwight's grandson for whom Camp David is named), a Churchill expert from Cambridge University, and Michael Allen, a UCLA prof who spoke about Celtic history. Alumni from Columbia, Cornell, Ohio State, William and Mary, the U. of Texas, Old Miss, and a coupe of other schools were on the Boreal with the 21 from UCLA (seven of whom were our clan).

Covering castles and gardens and wild highlands, then Trinity University in Dublin, and segments of Omaha Beach (including the American cemetery), in just six days, was a herculean campaign. It involved six different guides, a "steam" train, lunches and presentations in three countries, including an incredible men's choir in Llandudno, Wales.

In the evening, on the ship, we were entertained by French flavored dance revues (oo la la!) and an incredible Irish band and dance show. It was all quite exhausting, but more than redeemed by educational and entertaining quality.

The food was excellent—choice of two dining rooms—and the guidance was superior. The staterooms were a little tight for our taste and comfort, but Le Boreal is a relatively small and well-run French ship with a thoroughly international crew and flavor.

We have only a couple of suggestions for Gohagan Co.—they left us almost no nap or leisure time for a clearly elderly population—but as we rest and recover at home (at 91, I was, we believe, the oldest creature on Le Boreal), we do value the experience we had in just seven days and admire the organizational skills of Gohagan Co. I think all seven of our clan rate this expedition as one of our finest.

I should add as a footnote that not only was David Eisenhower an excellent lecturer, clearly a better orator and writer than his grandfather—the Allied Supreme Commander and the thirty fourth President of the United States—but he and his wife, Julie Nixon Eisenhower, are extremely down to earth and personable up close. Julie also spoke well in introducing David, who has always considered himself a writer first and educator second.

We are told that David's book, *Eisenhower at War* was a finalist for the Pulitzer Prize in History.

6/3/18

A First Hand Look at
"The Deplorables"

I SAT OUTSIDE A popular supermarket in Santa Ana on a Saturday afternoon at 2:00 P.M. I watched somewhere between 200 and 300 individuals, white, brown, and black, young and old, fat and thin, going in and out of the store.

After about 20 minutes I had to ask myself a question. Is this mob a fair cross section, random sampling of the American public in 2018?

I hope the answer is no, this is an atypical sample because middle America doesn't go out shopping in a chain supermarket on a Saturday afternoon—if only to avoid mixing with these specimens I have watched for half an hour now.

Genteel citizens would probably consider "slobs" and "goons" to be overly denigrating and hyperbolic labels when applied to such a large population. To the sensitive soul a "slob" must be conspicuously sloppy and unattractive, and a "goon" must be an individual who looks both stupid and menacing.

I'm sorry, my friend, but the mob I watched going in and out of this respectable supermarket in middle class America met one or both of these definitions in 80 percent of the cases. That's four out of five, or 160 out of 200.

Heaven help this nation if what I saw was a fair sample of the American electorate. And this survey took place in "Blue" America, where an articulate female attorney vastly out-polled an unhinged, vulgar blowhard a year and a half ago.

As a double check on my harsh assessment, I sat for another 30 minutes outside a flourishing Target superstore in the Irvine Marketplace an hour later. Again, mid Saturday afternoon in casual California, but in a more affluent neighborhood of western Irvine versus the supermarket in eastern Santa Ana.

Maybe there's a glimmer of hope on the horizon. But only a glimmer. "Slob" evolved to scruffy or sloppy-casual. "Goon" evolved to punk. The obese became more scattered. And the ethnicity changed from Latin and mixed to European and Asian.

So I guess the lesson for the day is what every Realtor and every sociologist knows. Location is primary and social class is critical. The bottom half of the herd isn't pretty. And the drama of human and social evolution is all too real.

6/16/18

WHO CAN ANSWER THE QUESTION?

A BILLION OR MORE Europeans and Asians are now asking themselves exactly the same question that sixty million Americans are asking each other: what can the United States of America do about a rabid, off-the-wall, out-of-control President and a cowardly, impotent Congress that is afraid to challenge him? Can the American republic survive another two years of a schizophrenic crusade against every figment of Barack Obama's legacy, against America's historic allies and trading partners, against scientific consensus, and against governmental curbs on abuse and corruption?

In fact, it would be fairly accurate to describe Trump's tweeted campaign as being hostile not only to the media and his critics, but to most functions of government per se. He has always spurned regulation and control and was schooled to be a street fighter by his indulgent father.

Sadly, we might not recognize American credo

and culture in two more years if Trump succeeds in 1) stacking the Supreme Court with right wing ideologues like Gorsuch and Kavanaugh, 2) withdrawing the U.S. from every treaty and alliance since WWII (TPP, Paris Accord, Iran, NAFTA, NATO), 3) continuing to dismantle every governmental protection against corporate fraud, environmental devastation, and governmental corruption, and 4) continuing to breed distrust of the press, the courts, the political process, and anyone who's not a Trump fan.

The fact is that the U.S. is in the hands of a one-man wrecking crew who can do grievous long term damage if left unchecked. He can't "Make America White Again" and he can't wall off the country's ten thousand miles of border, but he can repeal or undermine a lot of social and cultural engineering (with Gorsuch and Kavanaugh help), and he can continue to lower the moral and social ethos of the population with his continuous stream of xenophobia, paranoia, prevarication, and racial innuendo. His tough guy, give-em-hell, paranoid persona is already being reflected in his fan base in Red America, and polarization now existing between Red and Blue America will probably persist for years, if not a generation.

What is the answer to the world's question? What can America do about its half-baked, unhinged Chief Tweeter and Bully in Chief? I don't know the answer—unless a blue wave this November turns the

House of Representatives around and gets Congress functioning. But with a certain Republican Senate the odds of a recall would still be slim. And that wouldn't solve the critical SCOTUS problem unless one of the right wing court majority dies and a Democrat gets elected to replace Trump in 2020.

I'm not betting the plantation on a blue wave, a SCOTUS demise, or a Democratic replacement. I'm afraid the Democratic party is in tatters and both Elizabeth Warren and Bernie Sanders will keep it that way. Neither is the right candidate but they will muddy the campaign.

If you have a solution to the Trump Tragedy, come on over and have some vintage single malt scotch straight from the distillery. If you don't, my suggestion is a lot of British television—start with Poldark, Shetland, DCI Banks, and Inspector George Gently—and reap some more gains in the ridiculous Trump-fueled stock market.

7/16/18

Gentrification En Route to Emasculation

Let me be the first to predict that the flourishing campaign by feminists and their cadres of "exploitation" victims will lead ultimately to some grave injustice and some unappealing consequences.

The first aspect of the "MeToo" movement is that the masculine aggression complained of usually goes back years and years, often decades, to another era in human sexual history. The fact is that the code of sexual conduct has changed radically from the caves in southern Europe to the Victorian Era of the late 19th century to the Roaring Twenties of the early 20th century to the post WWII "sexual revolution."

The 7 ¾ billion humans milling on planet earth are proof that both men and women have always sought coitus under one sexual code or another, and until recently it was assumed that males would make advances on females they found attractive, to the point where the female drew a line in the sand.

Passing that point was always taboo, as offensive or even a crime. But until this century sexual innuendo or banter, or even solicitation, was not a stain on a male's character or reputation—because that's the way normal, healthy males are, and women learned to deflect the advances until the time was right.

But what has happened, and now has males in lofty positions under a bright floodlight, is a sharp change in the rules of sexual conduct, incited by victims of gross sexual aggression and fanned by angry feminists who have their own axe to grind against males in general.

What was sexual aggression short of physical force thirty or forty years ago is now classified as sexual exploitation even if no genitalia were involved and even if the "exploitation" was purely verbal or attitudinal.

This is not fair play and reminds me of a legal prohibition against ex post facto laws and indictments. In other words, you can't make something a crime, or even a civil wrong, by changing the rules and criminalizing or demonizing activity that was not illegal or immoral years ago. It's basically changing the rules of the game—in this case the sexual energy and activity game—in the middle of the game, without fair notice of the new rules.

My advice to the feminists and their victims, and to corporate Boards of Directors and Human Resource

Directors, is to start with section 9 of Article I of the U.S. Constitution and not make any ex post facto rules, then to evaluate claims of "sexual exploitation" victims in the context of what was accepted, or at least tolerated, sexual aggression in the era complained of.

Right or wrong, overt sexual aggression, even verbal or lightly physical, has now been dubbed taboo by a rising female chorus. Coitus and genitalia are out of the picture, as is any type of foreplay. Testosterone must be caged and even hands and lips confined. Keep at arm's length and don't talk dirty.

Call this new code gentrification if you wish. Call it a higher code of social behavior. But, thinking as a male, as I always have, I see the shift as another level of emasculation of American society. And as an ex post facto code grossly unfair to any male target who never went past the line in the sand drawn by his female accusers in years past.

8/3/18

A Quest for Serenity

YALE UNIVERSITY OFFERS A course for undergraduates entitled "How to Be Happy" or something like that. It's the school's most popular course. Apparently college students suffer serious depression today.

I don't know what they tell young adults except to cultivate and maintain personal relationships and to stay physically active.

But they are talking to youths just finishing adolescence who have their adult life yet ahead of them, with all the trials and tribulations—and lessons—of adulthood.

If I were offering that class to 80 and 90 year olds, I think it would have a different theme, although personal relationships and physical activity would still count.

Assuming that my senior audience has stayed alert and perceptive for 60 or 70 years, having seen trends, fads, movements, regimes, concepts, and administrations come and go, and having read widely in diverse non-fiction, my advice for being happy would be fairly simple: 1) turn off your intellect for awhile, focusing only on the here and now, and 2) turn off your insight into the future, which is apt to be grim if you're bright enough to be in my class.

The key to a bright veteran's serenity is therefore to turn off both any pain of the past and any vision of a grim future, and to focus on and soak up a cozy or ebullient presence. Alcohol or something chemical may be required by some. Some form of physical stimulation also helps to focus the brain on the here and now.

However, an aged Pollyanna or a cockeyed optimist wouldn't need this advice, having seen both the past and the future through rose-colored glasses. But such a goofy dweeb probably wouldn't be taking my class, anyway.

8/26/18

ARE THERE TWO AMERICAS? OR THREE?

ONE OF MY THEME songs, since I went from Stanford to Texas, then to Korea and Japan with southern and hillbilly rednecks, has been that there are really two Americas, one made up of middle class educated Northerners and the other made up of semi-literate, provincial yokels from the South, Appalachia, and the Texas-Oklahoma-Arkansas cowboy country.

The Blue States, consisting of the entire Pacific Coast and the East Coast from Maine to Virginia, was "our" world and the rest was "flyover country." After all, we had the *New York Times*, the *Boston Globe*, the *Philadelphia Inquirer*, the *Washington Post*, *The Los Angeles Times*, the *Portland Oregonian*, and the *Seattle Times*. We had the Ivy League and Pac 12 universities.

OK, the *Chicago Tribune* and the Big Ten schools did belong in our "America," but not much south of Champaign-Urbana, Illinois.

Yes, we did get six U.S. presidents from redneck

America—Truman, Eisenhower, LBJ, Carter and two Bushes, but none of them changed the America we knew in ways that upset us very much. Our courts, our press, and our schools were never attacked or undermined. America remained the light of the world.

Then came the November, 2016 bombshell. An unprincipled, unhinged, uncultivated con man put us in shock, took over the U.S., and began to dismantle the government that FDR, Ike, JFK, LBJ, and even Nixon had put together since The Great Depression and WWII. He and his wrecking crew, many already corrupt in private life (Tom Price, Scott Pruitt, Betsy DeVoss) began to repeal any and all environmental and commercial regulations, and international accords, set up over decades to fight commercial corruption and environmental degradation.

He packed the courts with right wing ideologues (like Gorsuch and Kavanaugh). He attacked the press as mendacious because it challenged him. He sponsored a new code of social conduct based on lessons he got from his father and attorney Roy Cohn (of McCarthy Committee fame). Attack, distract, then attack again. Mock and demonize your critics. Pretend you represent the forgotten poor white American. Promise to bring back that decent, God-fearing, country-loving white America.

Those of us in Blue America watch the crowds at Trump's endless rallies. Even though most of them are held in Red America, how can those thousands of Americans be conned by a man Michael Bloomberg long ago described as a true New York "con man"? He couldn't care one whit about those beaming and clapping rednecks—the same ones you would see at a World Wrestling match or a NASCAR race or a Demolition Derby or a Monster Truck rally or a UFC contest.

There are literally millions of them in this country. The polls still show a steady stream of support for Trump after two years of behavior that reveals him for what he really is, a semi-literate, corrupt, unprincipled blowhard who is making the U.S. both the laughing stock and a black sheep in the global showcase.

Are these millions of Americans completely out of touch with Blue America and the world around us? Do they really think we can withdraw from all international agreements and reject all scientific technology in this shrinking planet, then defend the U.S. against all comers?

Either Red America has descended into thirty or forty million yokels, rednecks, and hillbillies, or we have THREE Americas in North America—an educated and enlightened Blue America, which recognizes a rapidly shrinking and afflicted world, a Red America that thought Trump might solve some serious economic problems in an ever-more-competitive global trade battle, but now knows better, and a third isolationist, unsophisticated, anti-intellectual segment that will be Trump fans to the end.

We'll know more in four weeks. The only hope for a brighter American future lies in the disillusionment of millions of decent souls in Red America who turn on Trump's America at the polls in November. Even if that occurs, it will take years to salvage a severely damaged Federal government and to counteract the right wing court packing that has gone on largely unnoticed (except for Trump's choir boy, Kavanaugh).

10/6/18

About the Author

ROBERT V. WILLS TRAVELED extensively as a youth because of a Naval Officer father and a travel-prone mother. Multiplicity also characterized his college years, resulting in three degrees after four universities. His final degree was in Law at UCLA. That led to two different legal careers, one as General Counsel and Officer of a Big Board corporation and the second as a medical malpractice trial lawyer with his own law firm in Southern California.

His first book, *Lawyers are Killing America*, was a plea for genuine tort reform in the U.S. His next two volumes, *A View From the Hill* and *Gaining a Little Altitude*, contain essays on myriad areas of the American social and political landscape, reflecting a unique and unorthodox perspective on the passing parade. This volume continues that process.

If you enjoyed the book, please consider leaving a review at the online book seller's page for the book.

www.ingramcontent.com/pod-product-compliance
Lightning Source LLC
Chambersburg PA
CBHW022006090426
42741CB00007B/908

9780996167598